# Wild Pitch

~

Frank Nunez

Copyright © 2017 Frank Nunez
All rights reserved.

ISBN: 1974358151
ISBN-13: 978-1974358151

LCCN: 2017912813

BISAC: Drama / General

# Contents

Prologue ............................................................................. 1
Chapter 1 ............................................................................ 7
Chapter 2 .......................................................................... 20
Chapter 3 .......................................................................... 35
Chapter 4 .......................................................................... 49
Chapter 5 .......................................................................... 60
Chapter 6 .......................................................................... 71
Chapter 7 .......................................................................... 79
Chapter 8 .......................................................................... 87
Chapter 9 .......................................................................... 93
Chapter 10 ...................................................................... 103
Chapter 11 ...................................................................... 116
Chapter 12 ...................................................................... 126
Chapter 13 ...................................................................... 133
Chapter 14 ...................................................................... 144
Chapter 15 ...................................................................... 160
Chapter 16 ...................................................................... 175
Chapter 17 ...................................................................... 182
Chapter 18 ...................................................................... 199
Chapter 19 ...................................................................... 208
Chapter 20 ...................................................................... 214
Chapter 21 ...................................................................... 219
Chapter 22 ...................................................................... 222
Epilogue ......................................................................... 225

# Prologue

It had been fifteen years since I stepped onto the grounds of Tampa State, and just as many years since I put on a baseball uniform. Mist hovered over the grounds as I left my car in the empty parking lot. Through it I could see the silhouette of Brass Field, a ghost from a past that seemed so long ago. I lingered on the edge of the grass with a lump in my throat. The hairs on the back of my neck stood while I tried to embrace the nostalgia that hit me like a ton of bricks. I mustered up enough courage to walk through the early morning mist where the field became visible. The ping of metal bats and the popping of leather mitts echoed through the morning fog while the sun rose and evaporate the murky haze.

Practice just started within the confines of Brass Field. Players amble onto the field and began to catch, throw, and hit their way through their demons. A lifetime's worth of questions ran through my mind as I admired the brick façade of the administration building, with its silver domes fading from the heat of the Florida sun.

After spending most of the morning walking around campus, I ate lunch at the cafeteria where some of the guys and I used to shoot the shit and talk baseball and other nonsense. I could relive those conversations in my mind. I smiled at the innocence of it all. I never have conversations like that anymore. Whenever someone talks to me, I can only hear the drone of their chatter, an endless barrage of meaningless small talk numbing my mind while I would gaze at their forehead. I imagined I was somewhere else while I nodded and pretended to give a shit.

In the afternoon I continued my stroll around campus, following the path through the park, enjoying the shade underneath the trees, still as vibrant as I remember them. I walked through the cement pathway, which circled the park where there were benches, water fountains, and a variety of flowers and trees.

This was the same path Alison and I would take on lazy afternoons. Those moments seem so perfect when I thought I got it right. When life felt good and made sense. I felt light-headed and sat on a nearby bench. I sunk my head beneath my knees, running my hands through my hair hoping I could brush off the pain and anger that dwelled inside of me. I waited for a few minutes before I continued my stroll.

At the end of the park was the Hillsborough River with a view of downtown Tampa, the reflection of its' skyscrapers dancing on the water below. To my right was a dock with rows of boats of all types.

There were fishing boats with faded paint and odd names adorning their hull like "this one's for you" and "affair of the heart." Owners sat on their decks and enjoyed early morning drinks, a few watching a sailboat drift down the river, passing a rowing team finishing their morning rounds.

The wood of the dock was frail and worn, creaking whenever you stepped on it, while the boats swayed back and forth, smacking the dock with their hull. Beside the dock was a white storage shed riddled with bird shit and rust, but large enough to house all the rowing team's equipment. I took a girl there once named Brianne when I was a freshman. We met at a frat party and she was the first girl in college who would actually talk to me.

I never liked her very much. I was drunk and to be honest she was the only interesting person at a party filled with not exactly the best and brightest Tampa State had to offer. Brianne was a pre-law student who spent most of her high school years playing the valedictorian and honors student. She never did a bad thing her whole life. I was just an excuse for her to let off steam. I suppose that's what college is for.

The rowing team was prepping for an afternoon run. They looked so young and carefree. I envied them. Wishing I were on one of those boats and just sail away and forget who I've become.

In the middle of the bay was a small sailboat with an American flag fluttering on its' mast. A man wearing only shorts, his beer belly sticking out stepped onto the deck as he yawned and stretched. He scratched himself and grabbed a beer from the cooler next to him. He chugged it down and did martial arts moves to the sound of reggae music blaring from a cruiser close by. I chuckled, watching him until he stopped and sat to enjoy the view. I joined him as if I was seeing the gulf for the first time. I leaned against the metal rail, not taking my eyes off the man.

My anger for Bryce was still there, even as I absorbed the tranquility of watching the waves splash and sizzle against the wooden dock. The rowing team disembarked, the rowers' muscles stretching and glistening beneath their sweat and the Florida sun. A girl in a Tampa State shirt jogged passed me. Her dirty blonde hair was tied in a bun and her blue eyes glanced towards mine. Her perfume reminded me of Alison. For a moment, I thought it was her. I turned my head and almost grabbed her arm before I realized it was an impossibility. The brief sensation of euphoria vanished, returning me to the state of mediocrity that defined my entire life.

I returned to Brass Field, now against the backdrop of the new dorms being erected on campus. The field was just as I remembered it. The racing green of the outfield grass was rich and lush contrasting with the blandness of the infield dirt. Brass field wasn't as fancy as some of the fields of larger schools. Right field had a slight incline, which made tracking a line drive more difficult than it should be. The dugouts sunk below the field like a trench in WWI, and rumor had it the water fountains hadn't been working since the Roosevelt Administration. Even the third baseline, if you measured it, wasn't lined up with home plate. I'm not sure how the field passed NCAA standards, but it had its' own charm.

When practice ended, I sat in the grandstand. Alison sat in the last row on the first base side. I could still see her sitting and reading her book. It used to annoy the hell out me how she would stuff her face in them. There were times I would stay in her dorm and she would spend more time reading than having an actual conversation with me. Oddly enough, that was one of the reasons I was attracted to her.

Tucked behind the clubhouse sat the storage shed, the doors swaying gently in the breeze. I peeked inside and found a pitching machine, buckets of used baseballs no longer pearly white, and some mitts, dusty and worn with the leather stitching unraveling at the seams. I wondered if it was still here. I searched through several boxes of equipment, scanning the empty shelves until I noticed it sitting on top of the pitching machine. I picked up the radar gun, my body quivered as I sucked at my teeth just staring at it, recalling the memories, the anger, the hate that consumed my last few years at Tampa State.

I squeezed the trigger and smacked it several times before it turned on. The red digits zero, blinking at me in a mocking fashion. My body swayed like I was about to faint. The rush of memories hit me all at once.

I tried to forget the person I became all those years ago. My hate turned inward; consuming me the way the dirt had consumed the spilled blood after my actions on Brass field.

I kept asking myself why I came back. Maybe reminiscing was a way to bring peace. But deep down, I know I came back to rid myself of the secrets that haunted me for too long, the secrets that have scarred me beyond repair.

I missed the adrenaline, the feeling of stepping onto the mound and facing a hitter, hurling the pitch to home plate and hear the umpire yell, "Strike three!" Now I watch the game on TV at some neighborhood dive bar the world forgot. I sat alone even if it was crowded. I preferred to wallow in my own self-pity and relieve the glory days in the privacy of my alcoholic bliss.

Sometimes I wondered where Bryce was. The last I heard he played semi-pro ball up north. I felt both satisfied and disappointed in his fall from grace. A guy who was a certified major leaguer now played in some grapefruit league kidding himself about his chances of making it to the show. I could still see him when I close my eyes. God did I hate him.

Bryce might as well be a ghost. Just like Alison. She was probably married by now, or at least with a man far better than me. Even when we were together, I never felt I could live up to her expectations. Nothing I did ever seemed good enough, for her or anyone else.

The weight of the radar gun felt like a ghost in my hand. I placed it back where I found it and left the shed, strolling around the outskirts of the stadium until I noticed the gate to the field was open. It creaked as I shoved it aside. I felt adrenaline run through my body as I walked to the mound. I ran my shoes through the coarse dirt. The field showed signs of neglect. The outfield grass looked like it hadn't been mowed in weeks, and the infield dirt felt firm and dry like a desert with no oasis in sight. Coach Dawson would have a heart attack if he saw the field in this condition.

I stared down at the backstop, lining up to face an imaginary hitter. My back foot pressed against the rubber. I lifted my front leg, taking a long stride and whipped my arm forward, throwing an imaginary pitch. I made my way to the backstop and stood at the right side of the plate.

I hoped the pain would go away so I could find peace. I felt faint as a crisp wind from the gulf swooped in, and with it, all the overwhelming memories came flooding back.

# Chapter 1

The cool breeze from the bay struck my face with a soft and gentle touch that eased the pain in my legs from our early morning run.

It was six a.m., a late start for us. We usually began our run at five in the morning, but I slept in a little after a study-filled evening preparing for the afternoon's calculus exam. I groaned inwardly, cursing at Bryce underneath my breath with every step on the pavement of the Tampa State track, our substitute training ground during the off season when the baseball field was off limits, even to those on the team. Coach Dawson revered James Brass Field as sacred ground, guarding its manicured grass against violation.

"Come on, you can run faster than that," Bryce yelled as he inched ahead of me, toying with the preposterous idea we were athletic equals. Bryce was an impressive athletic specimen. At six foot three, two hundred plus pounds of solid muscle, his biceps bulged in almost any shirt he wore. Bryce was lean without an ounce of fat. Dirty blond hair, hazel eyes, he looked like he could have been a model for Abercrombie & Fitch. It was nauseating to be friends with someone who seemed so perfect.

His father pitched for the Texas Rangers for four years in the 80s.

A photo of his dad in the stretch posed in a wooden picture frame on his night table in Orsini Hall. Bryce played quarterback for Plant High School. A strong arm and decent speed made him a deadly combination to schools in his conference. But, like his father, baseball was his true passion. Bryce was a catcher and a damn good one. He could have played any position, but he wanted a challenge and being catcher lived up to those expectations.

"One more lap, Coop," Bryce said as he sped up.

"Show off," I yelled back trying not to seem I was out of breath.

We sprinted the last lap. I made it halfway around the track before my legs buckled as I trudged the last few yards. We rested for twenty minutes before we ran up the stairs between the bleachers.

"I can't," I wheezed, almost regurgitating the protein shake I'd had for breakfast. I couldn't go on. No matter how much I tried my body wouldn't cooperate. It was a feeling of helplessness that made my relationship with Bryce so complicated. I resented him for being better no matter how much I tried to raise the bar. Bryce kept going for another fifteen minutes before he met me at the edge of one of the steps.

"You all right?" Bryce asked.

"Just sore."

"It's good to get sore."

"Not for me," I said.

"Pain is just a state of mind."

"Tell that to my legs."

We finished the workout with a light jog. It was a nice reprieve from a grueling workout. My body felt refreshed at the sense of accomplishment, but it only lasted a short while because I knew I could always do better.

The sun rose from above the smooth and frothy waters of the gulf. We stopped at the dock, where the rowing team was readying their craft for morning practice. Water splashed against the chipped, faded wood of the dock, the foam sizzling beneath the rising Florida sun. Bryce and I watched the sunrise as we caught our breath.

Orsini Hall was a brisk five-minute walk from the bay.

Bryce decided to take the stairs while I slumped into the elevator. The elevator shuddered, struggling to pass each floor. I waited until the steel doors opened to the narrow hallway leading to our dorm. I walked over the once white carpet now stained with beer and bodily fluids too disgusting to mention. The cedar brown walls were covered with graffiti. I was always surprised in how many different ways the word *fuck* could be use for.

I arrive at our dorm to find Bryce already there. The dorm was a mess with clothes, baseball gear, and condoms scattered around the floor.

The room was symbolic of our last ditch effort to preserve our adolescence. To the right was a small wooden desk with a lamp and stacks of books, remnants from my studying session the previous night. A poster of John Belushi from *Animal House* wearing a sweater with "college" sewn on it hung over Bryce's bed. A dusty TV Bryce's dad gave us we barely used sat on a small stand beside my desk.

The idea of having to become adults after graduation was a sobering reminder of how little time we had to use our youth as an excuse to do stupid things.

"Damn it, can't you keep your prophylactics in order?" I said stepping on what I suspected was a used condom.

"Why, you need some?" Bryce asked.

"No. I still have some thank you very much. Courtesy of Gladys."

"Has it been that long?" Bryce said with his mouth open.

"Gladys and me broke up only 5 months ago. Plus I focus more on quality rather than quantity. That's the difference between you and me," I said throwing a dirty shirt I picked up off the floor at Bryce.

I grabbed some clothes from the closet and took a quick shower. I dried off and went to shave. I wiped off the steam from the mirror and looked at myself, examining the freckles and brown hair I thought made me look too ordinary. I hovered just under six-foot. I had an awkward gait where it looked like I would trip over myself every time I walked.

I was an average physical specimen with a good arm and the emotional intelligence of a teenager more mature for his age.

Bryce was a handsome son of a bitch. I had to give him that. His emotional intelligence was that of a toddler but he made up for it with a sunny disposition. I wouldn't go so far as to say he was a typical dumb jock, but he flirted with the cliché.

Bryce was one of those types who seemed to have it easy, or somehow at least made things look easy. He wasn't a mental heavyweight by any stretch of the imagination, but he had an instinct for knowing exactly how to get what he wanted. He had swagger and confidence about him. Nothing seemed to faze Bryce. Failure was never something he concerned himself with. The thoughts of losing his dreams never scared him. Whenever I brought up the possibility of not making the big leagues, he would laugh like the joke was on me. Life seemed easy for Bryce, but I suppose it was easy when your dad ran one of the largest law offices in Tampa. If baseball didn't work out, Bryce was going to be taken care of. It was that easy for him.

My parents on the other hand were as middle class as they come. My dad, a CPA, convinced me that being a CPA was a sure-fire way to get job security. I majored in Accounting just to get him off my back. Dad never liked the idea of me wasting time with baseball because he never thought I was good enough, at baseball or anything else. I don't recall the man ever giving me a compliment his entire life.

Back in high school before every game I would check the stands to see if he was there. I would find my mom sitting by herself until the third inning when she left out of sheer boredom. The only time I saw my dad at a game was my senior year when I was playing against Jesuit, one of the top ranked high schools in the state. I was warming up in the outfield when I saw him leaning against the outfield fence facing right field. I waved at him. He didn't wave back and left after the first inning.

We won that game. When I got home to tell him he asked me why I didn't bother to mow the lawn before I left the house. I shrugged hoping he would let it slide. He motioned his finger at me to follow him into the garage. The corvette red lawn mower was ready and waiting for me in the middle of the garage. "Get to it," He said. No mention of the game. Not even a pat on the back. He went to the game not to cheer me on but to serve as a sobering reminder that baseball was a waste of time.

My mother was in the kitchen cooking dinner. I snuck behind her and wrapped my arms around her waist, my tears wetting her blouse. She played with my hair and kissed me on the cheek. "Don't listen to your father." She said as she handed me my glove that sat on the kitchen table.

I loved everything about baseball. It was an escape. The field was my sanctuary from the burdens of everyday life. When I was out on that field, I felt immortal, like I could be and do anything. I dreamed about playing in the major leagues. I made sure I played as hard as everyone else just so I could prove to the scouts I had what it took.

Bryce didn't need to try so hard. I hated him for that. He had confidence, a confidence I sorely lacked in many aspects of my life. I always felt there was quicksand beneath my feet due to the constant struggle I felt trying to stay afloat so one day I might secure my little piece of the American Dream.

Bryce let out a loud sigh as he stretched out on the bed to let the world know he was disinterested in immediate matters.

"From that sound I assume that means you will not be attending class today?" I said drying off my wet hair with a towel.

"I'll think about it," said Bryce.

"Why the hell do I tutor you?" I replied.

"Because you're my bestest bud in the whole wide world," Bryce said with a wink.

"You still didn't answer my question."

"I have a C. Isn't that good enough?"

"Borderline C. Coach wants to see Bs," I said.

"What else is new?"

I heard three raps on the door, Zach's signature knock to let us know he was about to grace us with his presence.

Zach played second base. Not the strongest arm or the best bat, but he was a fast little shit, fast enough to make him lead off. He was the unofficial captain of the Silverbacks. Zach was the voice of reason when chaos arose. But, he could also be the source of chaos. He almost got half the team thrown out of a bar after a brawl involving an FSU pitcher over the quality of light versus dark beer. Coach Dawson nearly tossed most of the squad before Zach convinced him, in a debonair sort of way, that he was defending the team's honor because us drinking dark beer night after night was one of the reasons we were on a ten-game winning streak. Coach Dawson, a tough but superstitious man, took Zach's argument seriously. Rather than suspending his best players, he made us run wind sprints in ninety-five degree heat till we puked.

"Gentlemen, how are we doing this fine morning?" Zach said, wearing a red silk robe like Jay Gatsby himself.

"Bryce doesn't want to go to accounting class again," I said.

"Who's to blame him? Why do you think I'm majoring in English?"

"You see, that's what I think. I should major in English," Bryce said.

"What the hell are you going to do with an English degree?" I replied.

"I'll be the next Ernest Hemingway, goddamnit."

"You can barely read!"

"Bullshit! One time I saw Bryce reading the back cover of a book in the library," Zach said.

"Bryce. In the library? You caught yourself in a lie. Bryce would never enter a library on his own initiative," I responded crossing my arms.

"If I recall, you were running late because you got in an argument with Ms. med student. I figured I was in the library, why not read something? Make sense, right?"

"You see, an intellectual giant in our midst," replied Zach. "Will you be joining us in the dining hall today?" "Got class in a bit," I responded.

"You and class. It's not going to kill you if you're a little late. A man's gotta eat."

"Cooper, listen to the man, he makes a good point," Bryce said.

It was a five-minute walk to the cafeteria. The five of us sat in our usual spot, which was near the flat screen where we could get our daily dose of ESPN. Most of the Silverbacks infield was in attendance, plus Miguel, the lone outfielder, wearing his pristine Army ROTC uniform with his chest sticking out just a bit more than the rest of us. We nicknamed him Rambo because Miguel was softer than baby shit, bursting into tears on several occasions when Coach Dawson yelled at him for missing the throw to home plate. How he survived ROTC was beyond me.

The conversation always turned to baseball. We lived and breathed it. It ran through our veins as the lifeblood of our very existence. Zach, always the mediator, soothing tensions between those of us who thought swinging on a 3-0 count was justifiable if you got the right pitch, while the most conservative of us vied for the walk. It wasn't about the games we won or lost, but the trivial little things that to most people didn't matter, but to us, it all added up to how we played the game.

For me, there was only one thing that mattered, and that was reaching ninety mph. I thought it was everything. I couldn't break eighty-nine mph. If I broke ninety, it would make all the difference. More strikeouts, more wins, and more attention from the scouts. One mph, some extra twitches of muscle fiber, made all the difference between good to great. Coach Wells, the pitching coach, thought I was a tad overzealous and selfish for being fixated on something so artificial. But it was the edge I was looking for.

Samson, our recently promoted third baseman, scarfed down at least three waffles before he had to remind me of the edge, waving one finger in front of my face with a sarcastic grin. I wanted to rip him apart with my knife.

"I have to say, Miguel, you look mighty handsome in your uniform today," Samson said with a goofy grin.

"What's with the insolence? We may have ourselves here the next head of the Joint Chiefs of Staff," Zach said.

Miguel, like his uniform, had an aura of pride he fiercely protected against the daily sarcastic jibes. "I don't see any of you signing up," Miguel retorted. "Don't you see what's going on out there? We're at war. Doesn't that matter to you?"

I turned to the TV to find a video of Saddam Hussein standing on a balcony firing a pistol in the air in front of a massive crowd. Another war with Iraq was becoming a real possibility. There was tension in the air. We all felt it. Miguel joined the ROTC when he was a freshman because he wanted to be a part of something bigger than himself. We respected him for that because none of us had any intention of signing up. But the war was on everyone's minds.

"When you do think the invasion will start?" I asked Miguel.

"Not sure. I heard during the summer, maybe sooner."

"Will you be sent?" Zach asked.

"I don't know. I might be. I'm going to be an officer. They're going to need officers over there."

"Our little Miguel is all grown up," Samson said wiping away fake tears.

"Shut up!" Miguel replied.

"Why the hell are you people talking about this shit?" said Bryce. "We got a baseball season ahead of us, and you're talking about something that hasn't even happened yet."

"It's bound to happen sooner or later," I said.

"Even if it does, it doesn't make a difference. It's all bullshit anyway. It's all about money. Some old jerk wants to start a little war so he and his buddies can get rich. You know something, the whole thing is staged."

"Staged?" I said.

"Yeah, I mean think about it. War brings ratings, right? So the media and the White House cook up this little fake war. Use computer graphics and actors. A war will boost ratings and help the Prez with his poll numbers. It's like that movie, *Wag The Dog*."

"Are you that out of touch with reality? Are you even aware of what's going on out there?" I asked.

"Look, I'm just saying I'm a skeptic, okay? What we should focus on is the season and our first game against Eckerd. Agreed?"

Miguel picked up his tray and left in disgust.

Bryce looked at us. "What did I say?"

"You might as well have just spat in his face," I said.

"Oh Christ, Mr. Sensitive."

"Boys, as much as I would love to talk about geopolitics, I have biology in ten," Zach said, swallowing the rest of his eggs.

Samson finished the last of his waffles and looked at my plate of eggs. "You gonna finish that?" I took a big forkful and shoved it in my mouth with a grin.

Samson laughed and left Bryce and me to finish breakfast. "How did that kid become our third baseman again?" I asked Bryce.

"Because he hits the ball a ton and he can actually make the throws to first, unlike Balducci. He couldn't throw if his life depended on it."

"True. Are you going to Accounting or what?"

"Fine, Dad. Let's go."

After class, we hit the cages near the football field. The football players marched towards the practice field, eyeballing us as we reminded them of the coming spring. After our tee-work, Bryce put on his catcher equipment, and we made it out to the softball field so I could throw some bullpen. "I'm going to make you into the best damn pitcher this school ever had."

"I thought I already was," I replied.

"No. You're not," Bryce said, grumbling.

I made an artificial mound with some of the dirt from the infield while looking wistfully at Brass field across the way. The ball jumped off my fingers and popped Bryce's mitt. Dust billowed from the web of his glove, creating a small cloud around his mask. I picked up the balls one by one from the rope bag that lay next to my feet. I wound up and threw with authority. *Pop pop pop.* I launched my arm through the air like a whip, breaking the wind beside my face.

"That was not ninety," Bryce said.

"How do you know?"

"I could tell. You just know when the ball pops the mitt. You can feel it."

"Feel this." I wound up and threw as hard as I could. The ball sailed over him, flying over the fenced backstop.

I threw my glove to the ground in frustration.

"Oh, I felt that all right." Bryce laughed. He jogged over and patted me on the back. "Hey, you have to relax out there. You're too hard on yourself. Lighten up."

"Were any of them ninety?"

"Sure."

"You're not being serious."

"How the hell am I supposed to know? I'm not a human radar gun. Maybe they were, maybe they weren't."

There was only one radar gun we knew of, and it was in a storage shed beside Brass field.

"It's locked," I said, pulling the door.

Bryce jingled out his keys with a stupid looking smile on his face.

"Since when did you get a key to the storage shed?" I asked.

"When I took it off Coach Dawson's desk."

"Dawson's gonna be pissed."

"Hey, what's more important, breaking ninety or Coach Dawson's feelings?"

"Get the gun."

After smacking it a few times, the red digits lit up. We walked back to the field.

"Hey, wait a minute. Who's going to hold the gun?" I said.

"Well, damn, genius, you're the honors student. You should've thought about that before," Bryce said.

"Sorry," I said, embarrassed.

Bryce grabbed a water bottle from his duffel bag to get a drink when his eyes squinted. "Ask her?" Bryce said, pointing towards bleachers. When I turned I found a girl sitting on the bleachers reading a book.

"She won't know how to use that thing."

"It's not rocket science. You point and press a button. I thought you were all for women's lib, anyway?"

"What?"

"Because she's a girl she can't handle a radar gun?" Bryce smirked.

Her presence didn't seem to fit in with her surroundings. She didn't appear to be an athlete. I looked at her again. She was slender but well proportioned. Her face was covered by a copy of *Catcher in the Rye*. I walked over to her.

"How do you like the book?" I asked. I startled her a bit, making her drop the book. "Sorry, I didn't mean to scare you." She turned to face me, her left eyebrow raised and biting her lip as if she was trying to hold back saying something offensive. She wasn't wearing any makeup, but she beamed with radiance from her hazel eyes. She sighed, picked up the book and put it face down on the bench and crossed her legs while twirling her left foot.

"That's okay. My second time reading it. Salinger is one of my favorites."

"Why aren't you in the library or something?"

"I like changing my surroundings. Hey, what's that?" she asked, pointing to my hand.

"A gun… I mean—"

She jumped off the bench with a look of sheer terror.

"A gun! Oh my God, you can't bring a gun on campus. What do you have the gun for!?"

"No, it's not that kind of gun. It's radar gun." I said with my hands out motioning for her to sit back down.

She lowered herself back onto the bleacher. "Radar gun? Like the ones the police use?"

"Pretty much. I was hoping you could help us with it."

"With what?" she asked with a raised eyebrow.

I pointed to Bryce, who waved back with his mitt while adjusting his cup with his throwing hand.

"Bryce and I play baseball for the Silverbacks. I'm a pitcher and I was hoping you could use this radar gun so I can track my speed."

"I hate baseball," she said bluntly.

"Why?"

"Because it's boring."

I convinced her it would be easy, and it wouldn't take up too much of her time. She followed me to the artificial mound.

"Little small for a baseball field, isn't it?" she said.

"What's your name?"

"Alison."

"I'm Cooper, but everyone calls me Coop. This is Bryce."

"Coop over here is quite the feminist," Bryce quipped.

"What?" Allison said.

"Forget it, it's an inside joke," I said.

I gave her a quick tutorial on the radar gun and lined her up behind the fence near the backstop. I jogged back to the mound. I threw a few warm up pitches, irritated at the grin behind Bryce's catcher's mask. I dug my cleats in the dirt, pouncing on it like I was beating a dying animal with my feat.

"Ready."

The first pitch flew high and outside. "Eighty-eight!" she yelled.

I fired more pitches, pushing my arm to the limit. "Eighty-nine!" She yelled.

My arm felt tense. I stretched a little to loosen it up. I cracked my knuckles and punched my mitt with a closed fist. The next few pitches bounced off of home plate. "Ease up man, you've already thrown over fifty," Bryce said.

"How fast?" I yelled at Alison from the mound, ignoring him.

"Eighty-nine." She said.

"Are you sure you're reading that thing right?" I said walking to her.

She turned the gun over to show me the digits that read eighty-nine. "Let's call it a day," I scoffed.

"Why do you want to reach ninety mph?" Alison asked as she handed me back the gun.

"You wouldn't understand. Besides, don't you hate baseball?" I asked.

"Well, I enjoy watching you boys in your tight little pants."

"Just to let you know, I'm not wearing a cup," Bryce said with a sly wink as he wrapped his arm over my shoulder.

"I can't take you anywhere," I said to Bryce.

Alison's smile left me dazed. I wanted to make her smile like that again. I was transfixed by her as she left the field.

"Cute girl," Bryce said tapping me on the back with his mitt.

"You could have been a little less crude."

"Buddy, we're ballplayers, not saints. Take it easy, huh? How's your arm?" Bryce said grabbing my arm.

"Fine."

"Make sure you ice it up." Bryce said pointing his chin at me.

"How do you think I did?"

"I've seen worse," Bryce said.

"Thanks for the boost in confidence," I said shaking my head.

"You did fine. You got good stuff. Throw that way this season and we'll be winning plenty of ball games. Just remember to—"

"Ice up the arm, got it."

It cooled down as the sun began to set on the horizon. Bryce left to return the radar gun to the equipment shed. I walked alone in the shadows cast by the trees around the field, and their shadows hid me from the burn of the sun as it set in the western sky.

# Chapter 2

Practice began at 5:00 am. We would meet at the indoor pool in the gymnasium in the athletic complex next to Brass Field. Coach Dawson was there at four a.m. on the dot. We debated if the man ever slept. He was already in his Silverbacks uniform with an extra large cup of coffee from the school cafeteria containing enough caffeine to give any ordinary man a heart attack. Then again, Coach Dawson wasn't normal in any sense of the word. He was reserved, but possessed a quiet energy that kept us on our toes and focused on one thing: winning games.

He watched us swim laps, pushing us if he saw anyone slacking off. I wasn't a good swimmer. Few of us were. We were baseball players, for fuck's sake. He didn't care. He wanted endurance, strength, and speed. He wanted perfection in every sense of the word. I liked that about him. Coach Dawson was pure and authentic. You knew where he stood. I felt my legs cramp on my last laps. I thought I was going to drown.

"Keep moving, Coop. One more lap," Coach Dawson called.

I used my upper body to propel me to the edge of the pool. I swallowed a big gulp of water I began to choke on. Bryce waited for me at the edge of the pool, squatting with his hand out for me to take. He'd opened the slit in front of his shorts and pulled out one of his testicles with that Cheshire Cat grin of his. I glared at Bryce as I reached out and slapped his hand, considering where it had just been. He pulled me up from the pool as I coughed out the water swallowed. Coach Dawson's whistle blew like a freight train.

"Change up and hit the field," he yelled.

Brass Field was probably the most pristine baseball field on Earth as if the baseball gods had carved it out of grass and dirt. I admired the bronze statue of James Brass placed in front of the main entrance as I walked to the field. Brass was one of those ball players who became the stuff of legend. Rumor had it he struck out Babe Ruth four times during an exhibition game while belting three homers himself. At the time Brass broke every single college hitting record before he was drafted and sent to Europe to fight in WWII.

He died in the Battle of the Bulge before taking out a German machine gun nest. His heroics on and off the field made him more myth than man, his exploits occurring in a time when there was still some mystery left in the world. It must be nice to be immortal, to be remembered for doing something great. The greatest casualty of life is dying and being forgotten like you never existed at all.

I touch the statue before every game and practice hoping to capture a bit of greatness.

Practices involved bullpen, batting practice, drills, sprints, and training regimens designed to get us in playing shape for the regular season. At 21 I was in the best shape of my life. I ate and trained better, Bryce made sure of that. I was in the top of my class. But that magic number seemed so elusive.

I threw long toss and some bullpen. The popping of the catcher's mitt was more satisfying than hearing a girl moan after orgasm. Coach Webb stood behind me as I threw all the pitches in my arsenal. He had a thick goatee moistened from the spit of the wad of tobacco he would chew like a cow would chew grass.

"Just throw like that during the season," he said spitting onto the ground.

"Think you can get the radar gun?" I asked.

"Coop. You're a finesse pitcher. You're not going to blow people away with your fastball."

"I just want to see if I've improved."

"You let me be the judge of that. That's what the school underpays me for," he joked.

After classes, I would hit the library and study. I couldn't get any studying done in my dorm because either Bryce was blasting something most people wouldn't call music or was fornicating with a freshman. It isn't easy getting some alone time when you're surrounded by testosterone-fueled athletes who only think about baseball and getting laid, not necessarily in that order.

Higgins Library, a square, five-storey building with 1950s architecture and few windows became an oasis from the distraction riddled dorm room. I chose a desk next to the window on the fifth floor where there was the least amount of people.

Homework comprised of doing present and future value problems for Principles of Finance. The problems were easy and boring. I looked out the window to the campus below. It was buzzing with students coming and going from various classrooms and administrative buildings.

In the reflection, I saw Alison studying at a table several rows to my left. She didn't notice me. Or maybe she did but didn't care to acknowledge my presence. Her hair tied in a bun held by a pink scrunchy. Her forehead focused on the material she was studying.

"Hey," I whispered.

She didn't hear me the first time. I wasn't sure why I was whispering since we were the only two people in our row. "Alison," I said louder.

She looked up and grinned with curiosity. "Fancy seeing you here. I didn't know ballplayers were studious."

"I guess I might be an exception. What are you studying?"

"I have a paper on Chaucer for my Lit class. What are you studying?"

"Principles of Finance," I said.

"No thanks. Me and math are not good friends," Alison said with a look of disgust.

"Mind if I sit with you?"

"Well, you seem harmless."

What started as small talk led to a long conversation. Alison's father owned a jewelry store off Dale Mabry while her mom was a manager at a bank. She went to Community College and got her AA before transferring to Tampa State. She was majoring in English but hadn't the faintest idea what to do after graduation.

"I'm sort of going to feel things out," Alison said, biting the end of her chewed-up Bic pen.

"Isn't there anything you want to do? "

"I'll tell you what I don't want, and that's to feel like I'm some cog in a machine."

"What do you mean?" I asked.

"Think about it. Since we're born, we're told what to do and not do. Go to college, get married, take out a mortgage and buy a house. Get a job we're probably going to hate. Make little humans. Make just enough money to eke a living so your kids can learn how to do the exact same thing you did that made you miserable in the first place."

"Kind of a pessimistic view, don't you think?"

"The whole Ozzie and Harriet thing is a bit old fashioned for me, that's all. And what about you?"

"What about me?"

"What do you want to do after graduation? You're a senior, right?"

"Junior. I have a few scouts looking at me right now. Coach tells me I have a good chance of getting drafted if I have a good year. If baseball doesn't work out, maybe work for one of the top five firms."

"A banker?' Alison asked.

"CPA, but close."

"Christ, you're better off with baseball."

"I like numbers.

"I like sex, but it doesn't mean I'm going to make a career out of it," she said with a playful smirk.

"What about you? You don't seem to have much enthusiasm for doing something with your life after graduation.

"No, I don't believe in any sort of ism."

"Don't you believe in anything?"

Alison winked. "You're looking at her."

Several hours passed before the library closing bell rang. We left to find a few students lingering outside. The quad, with its mixture of palm and oak trees, created a tranquil ambiance. As we walked through the campus grounds, the dorms and administrative buildings were aglow with their lights, which shined on the walkways that weaved through the campus.

She held her books tightly wound between her arms. "I could carry those for you?" I suggested before she held her books closer.

"So, you never answered my question."

"What question was that?" I asked.

"Why do you want to throw ninety so bad?"

"Oh. That," I said scratching my head.

"Is it that hard of a question to answer?"

"Have you ever heard of *The Razor's Edge*?"

"No."

"It's a book, based on the concept that just one decision, one moment, one tiny adjustment can change your life."

"And what do you hope to change by pitching ninety?"

"Attention from the scouts, for one. Plus we all need to feel like we're making progress somehow."

"You boys and your pride," she sighed.

"You think it's stupid, don't you?"

She shrugged. "No. I mean, we all have things we want, I suppose."

"What do you want?"

"Me, world peace."

"Seriously."

A bird flew from one of the nearby trees. She pointed at it as it flew away. "To be like that bird. To be free. Not beholden to anything or anyone. Just free."

"An idealist."

Alison motioned to her dorm. "This is where I get off."

"Can I call you sometime?" I asked.

"Ahh, the typical courting ritual. Fascinating," she said.

"You're odd."

"You seem to like it, though."

"Maybe. Can I call you?" I persisted.

"Well, you know where I live now. Just come by and see me."

"When will you be around?"

"That's what makes this fun," She said smacking her lips.

The first game of the season was against Eckerd College, a private school in St. Pete. It was also our first home game of the season. I asked Alison to come. She liked the idea of seeing me in tights, or so she said, but she never gave a definitive answer. After warm-ups, I searched for her in the stands

"Who are you looking for?" asked Bryce.

"Alison. She said she would be here."

"You two dating or something?"

"We're going out tonight. First date."

"Take her to Chuck E Cheese."

"Chuck E Cheese?" I asked, confused.

"Yeah. There's nothing girls love more than watching a guy destroy the dreams of young children by beating them in Skee Ball."

"Thanks for the advice."

"You warm?"

"Yeah," I said.

"Good. I want to see that curve of yours. Oh, and that change up. It's mighty sexy if you ask me."

"What about my fastball?"

"You're not going to blow people away with your fastball. Stick with your off-speed stuff. We'll use the fastball to throw them off." It was irritating how Bryce told me what to do, even though he was my catcher. Damn, was it annoying.

Coach Dawson was a man of few words. He met the team in the dugout and gave the usual "play your game and mental toughness" speech that lasted as long as it took to tie the laces of my cleats.

It was scoreless the first few innings. Bryce and I worked in unison as he gave me signals from my arsenal of pitches. The batters didn't touch my curve. My changeup fooled them. I only used my fastball when I had to. We went up one nothing into the ninth with one out. I walked the leadoff batter.

Coach Webb called time and approached the mound. "How's your arm?" he asked.

"Fine."

"Bisley's up. He's got two hits off of you today," he said before coughing from the large of wad of tobacco in mouth.

"Ever tried gum couch?"

"What are you getting smart?" He said wiping the spit from his mouth.

"I'm fine, Coach. I'll finish this one."

Coach Webb left me to finish the ninth. Bryce jogged back to home plate when I saw Alison sitting in the bleachers. A boost of adrenaline rushed through my tired body. My arm got a sudden jolt of energy. Bryce called a curve. I shook off the signal. He called for the curve again. I shook it off again. He then called for a change. I didn't bother shaking him off. I got in the stretch and threw a fastball on the inside part of the plate. Bisley hit a towering foul ball over left field. Bryce called time and jogged to the mound.

"What are you doing?" he asked, surprised.

"I want this guy."

"Not by throwing him fastballs. He's had your number all day. You throw him another fastball and the next one he hits might stay fair."

The count was 0-1. Bisley took a few practice swings and dug into the batter's box. I checked the runner at first. Bryce called for a curve. Alison looked on but with a disinterested expression. I got in the stretch and threw a rocket to home plate. It was enough for a pop-up that ended the game with a 1-0 nothing score.

Bryce met up with me after a talk from Coach Dawson at my locker.

"That wasn't a curve," Bryce said.

"It was a curveball that didn't curve. Not by best stuff. My arm was sore."

Bryce, with his big wad of chewing tobacco and big league chew bubble gum stuffed in his mouth, nodded and grinned with a slight bite of his lip. "Sure it was, bud. Sure it was."

After the game Alison and I went to get pizza at some hole in the wall near campus that served pizza the size of your face. The interior made you wonder how it managed to pass any health inspections. I considered Chuck E Cheese, but then I realized I was getting dating advice from Bryce and how absurd the whole idea was.

We didn't talk much at dinner. I looked out the window and watched cars pass by the Tampa State campus.

"This is awkward," I said.

"Why?"

"Haven't you noticed there is this silent awkwardness whenever two people go on a first date?"

"You think this is a date?" Alison said.

I stammered for a moment as if I'd never spoken to a girl before. "Isn't it?"

She bit into her slice of pizza. "Dates are overrated."

"So you've never been on a date before?"

"I've never said that. I just don't like the concept of a date. There's this pressure to impress the opposite sex by putting on this fake persona. It may work at first, but it becomes unfair when both parties end up showing each other who they really are. That's when relationships go wrong. So, I prefer that we don't call this a *date,*" Alison said.

"So, you think I'm putting on a fake persona?"

She pointed the leftover pizza crust at me. "You see, that's the thing. I'm usually a good judge of character, but you're a hard egg to crack."

"Why?"

"Because there's more to you than just being a ballplayer. That's the reason I even bothered to come out with you tonight. You have depth. I can actually have a conversation with you. You'll be surprised at all the bullshittery I've seen guys throw at me. I should write a book about it."

"I see."

"So. Do you have a girlfriend?" She said sipping her diet coke.

"I wouldn't be here with you if I had one."

She turned her head. "Bullshitery. Remember?"

"Right." I snickered. "We broke up 5 months ago."

"Why?"

"We were headed in different directions. She was going to medical school. That's all she seemed to care about. Plus talking to her was like talking to a brick wall. It wasn't exactly a stimulating relationship"

She licked the pizza grease from her lips. "I'm always up for some stimulation." She threw back her bangs and stared at me.

"Want to go back to my dorm?"

"Do you have a roommate?" I asked.

"She's rarely ever there. She spends most of her time in the library."

Alison's dorm wasn't co-ed. No matter, the girls that frequented the hallways leading up to her dorm room didn't seem to mind my presence, as if they were used to having guys come and go on a daily basis. Alison's bed was as hard as a rock. My arm was still sore as I lay in her bed. Alison came in, wearing a bra and black thong with a small playboy tattoo right above her waist. Her bangs hung over her blue eyes. She parted them with her hand and straddled me as she got on the bed. She took off her bra. Her breasts bounced when she adjusted herself and leaned over to kiss me. Her kisses were wet and good, addictive like a drug. My hand ran down her back, feeling the hairs stand from the touch of my fingers.

We went to sleep before she turned on the lamp on her night table and read *A Separate Peace* while I lay next to her.

"You finished Catcher?" I asked groggily.

"Yup," she said, shaking the book in front of my face. I wrapped my arms around her and kissed her behind the neck. She liked that. The moan was a giveaway.

"I'm glad you made it out to the game today. I didn't think you would show."

"I'm full of surprises," she said as she was reading.

"Can I tell you something?"

She placed the book on her night table and examined me as she put her head on my chest. "What?"

"It was in the ninth inning when I first saw you in the stands. Bryce was calling for a curveball."

"What's a curveball?"

"It's a pitch."

"Oh. Well, go on."

"Anyway. Bryce calls the pitches he wants me to throw. He called for a curve, but because of you, I threw a fastball when I wasn't supposed to."

"And you did this because of me?"

"Is it weird?"

"A little. I mean you sure have a weird way of flattering a girl, but coming from you, I guess I'll take it."

"You just do something to me."

"I noticed."

She kissed me on the neck. Her breath made the hair on my neck stand while she ran her hand through my hair. "How long have you known Bryce?"

"We were having so much fun," I sighed.

"Well he's your 'catcher', isn't he?"

"I've known him since freshman year."

"Oh. You two must be good friends."

I felt my erection become flaccid as the mood seemed to go sour. I stretched and stared at the ceiling. "He's my catcher. That's all there is to it."

She smiled and ran her hand down my leg. It wasn't flaccid anymore.

I left her dorm a bit after midnight. I entered my dorm and found Bryce lying in his bed listening to his headphones.

"Could you at least have taken a shower?" Bryce grimaced.

"What are you talking about? I did after the game."

"No, I mean after you had sex. You reek of it," Bryce said. "Oh, next time you take some of my rubbers, let me know. We're student-athletes remember. Condoms aren't cheap."

"They were laying on the floor. I didn't think you would notice," I said.

"How's Alison?"

"Fascinating."

"She's got this sexy bookworm librarian thing going."

"I guess that's one way to put it."

"Is she why you threw those fastballs?"

I couldn't understand how he came to that conclusion. "What do you mean?"

"Don't play stupid. You were showing off. You want ninety so bad you're willing to throw your arm out for the sake of some girl."

"You don't know what you're talking about."

"Hey, I get it. Sometimes girls get in our heads. I just want to make sure we're on the same page out there. That pitch could've cost us the game. Starting the season 0-1 would put you on Coach Dawson's shit list.

I ignored him and changed into sweatpants and a T-shirt.

"Are you listening to a word I'm saying?" Bryce said.

"Sure I am. I know what I'm doing out there. I put the time in at practice, unlike some people."

"Practice does more harm than good."

"You can at least take it seriously."

"I don't need to. So, are we on the same page?"

I looked out the window, not wanting to hear his damn voice.

"Are we?" he asked again.

"Yes."

"Good. Oh, by the way, I'm going to need you to crash in Zach's dorm."

"What!? Why?"

"You think you're the only person having sex around here?"

"Come on. I'm exhausted."

"Can you just do me a solid? Brandon had to go home for a funeral. Zach should still be up writing a paper."

Zach's room was the antithesis of ours. It was kept clean and tidy. Both his and his roommate's bed were made with the sheets washed and crisp without the slightest crease or wrinkle to them. When I entered I was welcomed by meditation music blaring from his small speaker on top of his desk. I found Zach with his eyes closed sitting Indian style in a meditative trance, wearing only his boxers and white socks

He took deep long breaths, exhaling through his mouth and holding his breath for a few seconds before he repeated the process. I wasn't sure if he knew I was there. I waited for him to notice, but he continued his meditation, unaware of my presence. I hung by the door until he opened his eyes with a wide grin. He looked up at me and turned his head as if he never met me before.

"Why Coop, come in, good sir."

"I hope I'm not interrupting… ugh… whatever you were doing?"

"Oh. Sorry. I was doing transcendental meditation. Great way to relieve stress. You should try it."

"I don't think I'm much of the meditative type."

"Suit yourself."

Zach picked himself of the floor. He stretched his arms and put on his robe, exposing his abs through the open slit of it. "So what brings you to my humble abode?"

"I was wondering if I could crash here? Bryce is fornicating and I have no place to stay. He told me your roommate was out of town."

"Sure, but just to let you know Brandon has what you call a 'medical problem.'"

"What problem is that?"

"The kid pees his bed."

"Come on!"

"I'm not joking. I've seen it happen a few times. I think he told me it has something to with some personality disorder where he hasn't outgrown his inner child or some shit like that."

"Is that how Freud described it? I'm going to kill Bryce."

Brandon's comforter smelled like fabric softener. I lay on top of it to make sure I avoided the soiled bed sheets.

"Good game today," Zach said.

"Thanks."

"Wish I could say the same for me. I went 0-4. I keep this up Coach Dawson will move me down the lineup. Or worse. Sitting on the bench isn't how I want to spend my collegiate career."

"It's one game. Don't sweat it."

Despite the sheets beneath me, I got comfortable enough to unwind after throwing close to eighty five pitches. Zach continued typing before he turned to me. "You're hiding something, aren't you?" he asked.

"What are you talking about?" I asked.

"You know what I'm talking about."

"I don't, actually."

"Alison."

My curiosity peaked. "How do you know her?

"She's in my English two class. We're part of a three-member group working on a presentation for *A Separate Peace*," Zach said, showing me the worn out paperback copy he took from his desk with the spine peeling from its side, but the title of the book still visible. "I saw you two talking after class. Wasn't hard to figure out."

"Oh... right."

"You never told me about her."

"Was I supposed to?"

"You told Bryce though, right?"

"Can I go to sleep now please?"

Zach's lips squirmed as his tongue ran over its surface and he ignored my response. "Alison is a complicated girl."

"What would give you that idea?"

"Alison is what I would call a bohemian. A free spirit. She can't be tamed. Kind of like me," Zach remarked.

"And you figured this all out by working with her on some group project?"

"I'm good at measuring people."

"Have you measured me?" I asked.

Zach scratched his scalp, running his fingers through his black coarse hair, tapping the wooden desk with his trigger finger. "I'm not sure. Don't know if that's a good or bad thing," he said, amused.

"Good night, Zach."

Zach shut off the dorm light. The desk lamp was all that remained casting light on his work. I dozed off, hating Bryce for making me sleep in a soiled bed.

# Chapter 3

I went for a run alone. We had a day off. Alison went to visit her parents, and Bryce's knees were bothering him. There's nothing like going for a run on your own. Nothing to hold you back. You just ran.

It was a cool morning; a brisk breeze swept in. Something about the gentle wind gave me a jolt of energy. My mind and body flowed in perfect unison, my limbs pumping together like a well-oiled machine. I admired the scenery zipping past me until I reached Brass field. The sprinklers sprayed water onto the thirsty grass of the field, the mist spraying my feet as I jogged past the bullpen. The campus was eerily quiet as students would not awaken from their collegiate slumber for another few hours. A thick fog engulfed the campus. Anyone caught in it looked like a ghost amid the fog. I saw a ghost dance in the distance.

"Coop!" its voice yelled.

The ghost got closer. I became startled, because it could see me, but I couldn't see it. It's jumpsuit, black with yellow stripes with "ARMY" in big bold yellow letters stretched across the front of it, stood out in the soupy fog. I wanted to run in the other direction, away from the silhouette of a man who could've been anyone. I recognized the man exiting the fog.

"Miguel, soldier of fortune," I said.

"I thought I was Rambo?"

"That's what everyone else calls you. I'm giving you my own nickname."

"Thanks, I guess. Want to run together?"

I didn't want to. I ran with Miguel because he insisted. I was in better shape than him. I knew that I would have to slow down for him, but we ran together anyway for the sake of "team camaraderie." He kept up for a while, but struggled the last few miles.

"Hey, can we stop for a sec? I need a break," Miguel said.

We stopped at a large oak tree that sat on the outskirts of campus. The trees' leaves, each with its detailed green pigmentation, created a lush landscape between the College of Business and the Science Building. Beside the Science Building was a small pond; giving us a great view from the oak tree. I rested my back on it, its trunk, thick and true, displayed its ancient wisdom well before the construction of the university.

Miguel leaned over and spat out a large wad of phlegm. He rested on the tree's large, thick roots and leaned against the trunk, knocking down chips of bark. We enjoyed the early morning serenity through casual conversation and admiring the view of the lake, just taking it in with no sort of distraction from the day's usual routines.

"You ready?" I asked.

"For what?"

"For the war."

Miguel thought for a moment and stood up, plucked some of the bark from the tree. "I think so."

"You think so?"

"Sure. I mean, that's what they're training me for. The real training begins when I graduate."

"You think there will be a war?"

"As long as human beings have differences there will always be war," Miguel said solemnly. "You know there was a tree just like this one at a park near my house. I used to play in it as a kid. It was next to a lake in Winter Park. My brother and I used to go there and dive off the branches and into the lake. One day when my brother and I were on the branch, he just shoved me. I landed on the ground and broke my arm. I had to wear a cast for several months. Damn was my mom pissed."

"Why did he do that?" I asked.

Miguel pulled a leaf from a nearby branch. "I don't know."

"You don't know?"

He shrugged his shoulders. "I suppose he was just being a kid. But it's funny how we do things that seem to be beyond our control. Like there is this other part of us that wants to come out without our permission. Maybe that's why people do bad things, because we always have to fight that dark side of us. Anyway, I still talk to my brother from time to time, but we were never that close after that. He lives in Colorado, the last I heard from him."

Somehow, I understood what Miguel was talking about. We had much more in common than I first thought, and it scared me because he was right about the dark side within us. For sometime, I felt something pulling away at me. Torturing me from the inside, playing with my conscious and questioning my morality. I felt I was losing my sense of self.

I pulled more bark from the tree and threw it out over the grass. I sat next to Miguel on one of the large roots. "Do you think you could, you know, kill?"

Miguel shifted on the root and gazed out onto the campus. "I'll have no choice. But it isn't the killing I'm worried about. After we leave here, we have to go out into the real world. It's different out there. It's not like here, where you're protected, you know? Where if you fuck up you just get a bad grade. Out there, I don't know. Sometimes I wonder if I could take it. I guess that's why I joined the army. I want to prove myself." Miguel lifted his chin. "Out there."

Miguel pushed himself off the root. We both stretched before we continued our run. As we ran, I thought about what he said. Like the war, the real world was approaching, and none of us knew what was going to happen after we graduated. I always heard about how college would be the best time of your life, and it was all downhill after that. But I never understood that saying because I didn't feel like I was living in my glory days. I always felt my best effort was never enough. I was just good enough. I studied as hard as I could and I practiced even harder, but somewhere down the line, it never seemed like it would make any difference because there were others who seemed to catch all the lucky breaks. Those who had it easy. Those who got it all without trying.

Monday, I met Alison in front of the Liberal Arts College after class. She spent the weekend with her parents, which, according to her, was "infuriating". Reliving her childhood by staying in her old bedroom did not conform to her paradigm of liberation. "Did you tell them about me?" I asked.

Alison, puzzled, finished her bag of Skittles. "Why would I do that?"

"Well, I don't know."

She crossed her arms." Sure you know. You want to satisfy your primal urge to verify that I'm your property within the context of a monogamous relationship."

"English, please." I said with a confused expression.

"You're insecure." She said throwing a yellow Skittle at me.

"You got all that from me asking you if you told your parents about me?"

"Why would you care if I told my parents about you unless you wanted verification about our 'relationship'?"

"So we're in a relationship?"

"I don't like labels." She said shaking her head.

"So then, what would you call us?"

Alison popped her last green Skittle into my mouth. I held it between my lips. "I call it experimentation." She kissed me with her soft, moist lips, snatching the green Skittle wedged between mine. "See ya."

We hit the road for a 2-game series against Florida International. I pitched a gem of a game, striking out ten and giving up one earned run. Coach Dawson gave me a pat on the back and a smile, which was the most Coach Dawson could muster in terms of emotion. I slept a little on the bus ride back but felt sick from playing under the hot Florida sun. The heat can get to you. Bryce could sometimes lose five pounds in one game. He nearly fainted in a game against the Gators. Coach pulled him out after Bryce threw an absolute fit. He thought he was invulnerable.

Zach sat in the seat next to mine reading Vogue magazine. He preferred sophisticated women and enjoyed the subtle images of sexuality rather than the obvious images of the female body. "It's what you don't see that's sexy," Zach said. "It's the skirt that shows a little skin. Or the blouse that exposes some cleavage. Her killer smile. That's sexy," he exclaimed.

"Glad to see you have an excellent taste in women."

"I like quality over quantity. Unlike Bryce here."

"Shut up," Bryce said, with his eyes still closed in a meager attempt at sleep.

Samson popped his head over the seat in front of me. "Hey Coop, did you hit ninety today?"

"Not sure. Coach forgot to bring the radar gun again," I replied.

"Shame," he said. "I think you're funny."

"What?"

"You're obsessed with throwing ninety yet you hold yourself back in so many ways."

"How so?"

"You don't like to talk about yourself," he said.

"Maybe I just don't like talking to you."

"Oh, come on. I'm the only one here you can talk to." Samson leaned in and whispered,

"Everyone here is a phony. They pretend to be something they're not. You see, I am the genuine article. What you see is what you get. I don't hold back. That's the difference between you and me. So, if you want to throw ninety, you can't hold back. You gotta let it all come out. Know what I mean?"

"No. I don't."

Samson scoffed as I closed my eyes to get some sleep. It was a long bus ride back to Tampa.

Later that week Bryce woke me up from a deep, restful sleep. It was still dark outside. "Do you know what time it is?" I asked, perturbed.

"Early bird gets the big league contract, buddy."

"Do you ever sleep?"

"You'll have plenty of time to sleep when you're dead. Come on, it's time for our run."

"Fuck," I groaned.

"Come on, Coop, do you want it bad enough or what?"

To run while most of the civilized world was asleep wasn't very appealing after spending the previous night with Alison and playing a doubleheader that day. Coach had put me in right field. He didn't like pitchers sitting on their asses all the time on their off days. The sky was still dark. The crickets chirped like a finely tuned chorus while we ran through the campus grounds. Bryce began moved ahead of me. I pushed harder, but I kept losing ground.

"You're getting slower, Coop," Bryce said.

"I'm just taking it easy on you."

I ran faster, and Bryce noticed. Our jog turned into a sprint, side by side we ran as hard as we could. Brass Field was ahead of us. My lungs felt like they were ready to burst. Bryce inched forward. He gave me a wide smirk moving farther ahead while I pushed my legs into overdrive. He made it look so easy. I lurched forward, pumping my arms, our feet stomping the pavement in close proximity as I caught up to him. For a moment I lost control of my body. It wasn't long before our bodies collided. Bryce flew to his left and tumbled on the grass several times before he came to a halt while I regained my balance.

"What the hell are you doing!?" Bryce snapped as he dusted the dirt and grass from his jogging suit.

"Sorry."

"Sorry? I could have broken my neck!"

"Oh, please."

"What the hell were you doing?"

"I tripped."

"You tripped? Well, next time you trip make sure you don't take other people with you."

"Hey, you're alive. That's the important thing."

"Smart ass," Bryce said.

"Want to finish the run or what?"

"No more tripping."

"I promise."

We both ran off as I kept my fingers crossed.

I enjoyed long walks with Alison as cliché as that sounds. It was better than visiting bars on a daily basis like our fellow students.

Alison wasn't much into the dinner and a movie thing. One, because she thought cinema was dead, and two, because the best place to eat around campus was a Spanish restaurant that gave her food poisoning. The confines of the campus suited her fine.

We sat on a bench and admired the squirrels' skip over the grass with ease, climbing and leaping off the branches of the nearby trees.

"This is nice," Alison said.

"Yes, it is."

"How's the season going?"

"We're in first place. Wish you could make more of the games."

"I've gone to a few."

I snorted. "I count two."

"You're lucky I went to one."

"Sometime I wonder if you like anything."

"That's not true. I have distinct tastes. Speaking of tastes, I'm hungry."

"There's always the school cafeteria."

"How romantic," Alison said scrunching her lips.

"And some dive bar is better?"

"I know a place."

Le France was, as its name implies, a small French restaurant a few miles away from campus. Alison discovered it when her parents first visited her, the first and only time. Stereotypical French elevator music played as the waiter sat us at a table near the window that overlooked the highway. Alison studied the menu. Her mouth twitched as she looked over the menu.

The waiter took our drink orders, and brought us water, dinner rolls and butter. The pat of chilled butter melted on the warm soft dough of the bread.

"What are you going to have?" I asked.

She rolled her hair in a bun with a pink scrunchy she pulled from her brown leather purse. "Not sure."

"The chicken looks good," I remarked.

"Why, because of the price?" she said with a grin.

"It has lemon butter sauce."

"Don't worry, Coop. I'm not going to order the lobster, if that's what you're worried about. Besides, I'm buying."

She ended up ordering pasta. I got the chicken. The food was good. Better than anything around campus. She savored the pasta, taking in each bite.

"Dessert?" I asked.

"Later?" Her smile melted me like the butter on the bread. She grabbed my hand underneath the table, discreetly, not wanting to let on to anybody. Labels. *Sish*.

We made out in the car for a while before we drove back to campus.

"Let's go back to your dorm," she suggested. " I want to be close to you tonight."

"That's sentimental of you."

"I care for you Coop. I know I'm difficult sometimes, but that's because it's difficult for me to open up."

I ran my fingers through her hair and pressed my lips against hers, my blood warming to her sensual touch as her hand grazed my back.

"I never felt like this about anyone before," I said. "Is that weird?"

"No. I think it's authentic. A quality few people have nowadays."

I shook my head. "You and your philosophy."

I pulled her closer, pulling her hair as she kissed my neck.

"We should go."

"Um, yeah." She said with a seductive smile.

We made it to Orsini Hall. My dorm room window was dark. We kissed again on the steps before I grabbed my keycard.

"Get a room you two!"

Bryce had a way of making an entrance. Being subtle wasn't his style. Alison looked down in embarrassment.

"Nice to see you, Bryce." I seethed with annoyance.

Bryce winked and grinned like he always did.

"I thought you were out?" I asked.

"The day is still young buddy. I was just going back to change unless you two need some time alone." Alison crossed her arms with squinted eyes and scrunched lips.

"Alison, I'm sure you remember Bryce," I said.

"Oh yeah. The catcher, right?"

"Yup. I have to catch this bum every five days."

"You'll have to get used to Bryce's sense of humor. He hasn't developed his sarcasm yet, so he can be rather blunt."

"No shit," Alison said.

"Sarcasm is like fine wine. It gets better with age. Say, I was heading over to Chase's Wing House, why don't you two join me?"

"You were going by yourself?" I asked.

"I was going to meet with Zach and some of the guys but they bailed on me last minute."

"Well, we just ate."

"Oh," Bryce said, disappointed.

Alison stared the other direction while I debated what to do. She turned to me and laughed underneath her breath. "We'll tag along," She said.

We waited for Bryce downstairs while he changed. I scoffed at Alison.

"What? I feel bad for him." Alison said.

"Why?"

"Because nobody should have to go to a bar by himself. I think it's against the rules," Alison said.

"There are rules for such a thing?"

"There's the unofficial kind that aren't written in any sort of constitution, just passed down from one drinker to another."

"I learn something new every day."

---

Chase's was one of those generic sports bars with sport paraphernalia adorning every inch of its walls. The biggest draw was that the beer was cheap and the food was edible.

"Glad you guys came. I hope I wasn't interrupting your date."

"I like to call it a brief intermission," Alison said.

"Huh?"

Bryce, puzzled, finished his first beer and went for his second frosty beverage. "You sure you don't want a beer?" he asked.

"I prefer wine," Alison said.

"You don't like beer?"

"Does that surprise you?"

"I mean, well, most people I know like beer."

"I'm not like most people," she said.

"Ain't that the truth," I said.

"Oh, really?" Alison asked.

"I meant that in a good way. We're all different in our own way, right? If you don't like beer, fuck it, you don't like beer."

"I guess that's one way of putting it. I'll try some wings though," she said.

"Didn't we just eat?"

"I'm still hungry. The pasta didn't fill me up."

"Yes, Coop. The girl wants to eat. This guy must not be feeding you."

Bryce ordered a plate of greasy barbecue wings. I had one while Bryce and Alison devoured the rest. For a girl so small she could eat more than Bryce and me combined. "Now are you satisfied?" I asked Alison.

She grinned, sauce still smeared across her lips. "That hit the spot."

Bryce cleansed his palate with another beer. His lips were stained with barbecue sauce, too.

"So Bryce, how good is Coop?" Alison asked.

"At what?" Bryce replied.

"Well, pitching for starters?"

Bryce pouted and nodded his head. "The kid's got potential. He's good, but he could be a lot better."

"I have five wins this season!" I exclaimed.

"It ain't just about wins, buddy."

"And what about you?" Alison asked.

"What do you mean?"

"How good are you?" she asked, squinting her eyes.

Bryce took a sip of his beer and swished it in his mouth before gulping it down. "I'm better than most."

"Is that your attempt at modesty?" Alison asked.

"I would say I'm pretty damn good."

"Not the best?"

"Bryce led the league in RBIs last year," I said.

"Well, that's good right?"

"It ain't bad, sweetie," Bryce said.

"Oh, I'm not your sweetie," Alison replied.

"Sorry, sorry. You're Coop's sweetie."

"You boys are all the same," she said, rolling her eyes.

"Oh right, Coop mentioned you don't like labels. Whatever the hell that means."

Alison gave me a dirty look before turning to Bryce. "Like someone of your intellect would understand."

He finished his beer. "You sure know how to pick 'em, Coop."

"Hey, ease up, Bryce," I said.

"What did I do? She's the one that insulted me. I'll have you know I'm a lot smarter than you think."

Alison nodded her head as if she was agreeing with a child.

"You don't believe me?"

"I'll believe it when I see it."

"Hey, I don't need to be hearing this shit."

Alison grabbed her purse hung on the barstool. "I think it's best I leave. Bye."

I followed Alison outside. "Come on, don't leave."

"I can't deal with somebody like that."

"What do you mean, 'like that'?"

"This macho, meathead crap. I dealt with that in high school. And what have you been telling him about me…labels?" She said smacking my arm with the back of her hand.

"It just came up. And you don't gossip about me behind my back? Besides, Bryce is a good guy once you get to know him."

"I suppose." She looked dubious.

"You know, you don't have to get so uptight."

"This macho meathead crap gets underneath my skin, Coop. I Don't have the patience for it."

"Why don't we go back to my dorm? Bryce will be out late anyway."

"I'm not in the sentimental mood anymore." Alison pecked me on the cheek this time, leaving me with Bryce, who was watching ESPN on one of the bar's many flat screen TVs. "What was that all about?" Bryce asked.

"You just don't understand her."

"Like you do?"

"She's different."

"Well, she's bad news. A girl like that gives you nothing but problems. You don't need that during the season."

"She's not a problem."

"I'm your catcher. And I say she is."

He insisted on going bar hopping, as the night was young, but I preferred going back to the dorm. Bryce pouted at the thought of going home early, but refused to go drinking alone like a "damn fool", as he described it.

We walked past Alison's dorm. The light was still on. I wondered what she could be doing. I thought about seeing her but decided against it. I wasn't in the mood for drama.

Orsini Hall was quiet. It was Friday and most of its inhabitants were out. I enjoyed the silence. Bryce didn't notice those types of things. He was oblivious to the small nuances of everyday life. He focused on the big picture. A generalist at heart. He fell asleep. I was no longer tired, so I changed into my workout clothes. The night was cool and calm. I just ran, not wanting to think of anything else.

# Chapter 4

The game against Rutgers was delayed due to a thunderstorm that rolled into Tampa Bay. The lightning crashed in the distance. A rainstorm rumbled from the bay into the stadium as we waited in the dugout until the rain subsided. I sat at the end of the dugout while I watched the rain drip from the top of the dugout and splatter on the ground creating small puddles that grew as the rain intensified. Samson emerged from behind the dugout and sat next to me while he applied tape to the handle of his Easton metal bat.

"When did they say the rain would end?" He asked me.

"In half an hour."

"Half an hour! Are you sure?"

"I'm not the damn weather man. You can't wait half an hour?"

"I got a rhythm, you know. I don't want to lose it before the game," he said, twirling the bat like a baton.

"It's all in your head."

"Oh, so you're not a weatherman but a shrink now?"

"Samson, I'm not in the mood," I said.

Samson stood and put his foot on the bench of the dugout and leaned into me while he gripped the handle of his bat, admiring the stock of the barrel. "You don't like me too much, do you?"

"Seriously?"

"Yeah."

"What gives you that idea?"

"Because I get under everyone's skin. My own mother told me. Hard to believe huh?"

"Sure."

Samson applied one last stretch of tape to give him a good grip. He picked at a few of his blisters before he tried on a new pair of red and white batting gloves.

"Think you'll hit ninety today?" Samson asked.

"You might jinx it if you keep asking me."

"Wouldn't want to do that." Samson's smirk widened.

"I'll see ya on the field," He said moving to the other side of the dugout.

The rain ended, but the sky remained overcast and gloomy. The game started with me giving up four earned runs the first three innings. It was the fourth inning when I threw my mitt against the bench in disgust and paced back and forth cursing at myself. We were down four to one. Coach Dawson approached me as I watched Bryce's turn at bat.

"You feeling alright?" he asked.

"Just started off slow. I'll settle in."

"Okay. But another inning like the last one and I have to pull you."

"I'll finish this one out."

I lasted two more innings before giving up a two run shot in the sixth. When the game ended we returned the locker room. I peeled off my sweat drenched uniform and sat on the wooden stool while stretching my sore arm. Across the locker room Bryce glared at me, shaking his head as he took off his gear. I didn't return the look. If I did, I would have thrown the stool at him.

"Not your best stuff today," Samson said.

"No, it was not."

"It's the rhythm. I'm telling you."

I walked back to my dorm alone. Bryce was waiting for me outside of Orsini Hall.

"What happened today?" he asked.

"It was a bad day."

"No shit it was a bad day. Your stuff was horrible."

"We really doing this now?"

"You won't make the pros with that kind of pitching," he said with his arms crossed.

"It's one game, Bryce"

Bryce bit his lip and sighed like a father ready to chastise his son. He looked out over the quad and spit a wad of phlegm onto the ground.

"One game can make or break you. You know this. It's that girl."

"What does Alison have to do this?"

"That girl's messin' with your mind."

"You don't know what you're talking about," I said, shaking my head.

"Sure I do. I have nothing against her and all. She's just not for you."

"How would you know what's good for me?"

"Because we're like brothers, that's why. I'm your catcher. That means something." He said smacking my chest.

"I suppose it does."

Maybe you're right. It's one game. Don't make losing a habit."

"I don't plan to."

After our talk we grabbed dinner at the cafeteria and went our separate ways. I hadn't heard from Alison since the previous day. I knocked on her dorm room door. She opened it, her eyes half shut. "Get you in a bad time?"

"You should have called. I was sleeping."

"I was in the neighborhood. I wanted to see you."

"Come in," she said.

I leaned in to kiss her when I smelled her bittersweet strawberry perfume,. "I could come back. I didn't hear from you since yesterday."

"Sorry. I was busy with homework. I had a paper due today."

"Oh. I thought you didn't want to talk."

"Why would you say that?"

"About the other night."

"I guess I was sort of a bitch."

"I think it was just miscommunication."

"Maybe," she replied staring down at the brown carpet.

Her perfume lingered on my body as we lay together in her bed. I watched her sleep and played with her hair as the hours seemed to fly by. I ran my hand up and down her thigh. I kissed her on the neck. She opened her eyes. I rolled over and began to slide down her white thong when her elusive roommate came in, not even glancing at us as she went straight to her backpack that sat on a chair beside her bed. We shuffled underneath the bed sheets and composed ourselves.

"Did I wake you?" she asked, unzipping her backpack.

"Have you ever heard of the concept of knocking?" Alison said.

"Um. It's my room too. Why should I knock? Who the hell are you?" She said pointing her finger at me.

I shrugged. "Cooper."

She picked up some books, shoved them in her backpack and bolted out the door without saying a word.

"I don't think I made a good impression."

Alison sighed. "She's OK. I don't think she's seen a boner in a while."

"Come on. We can get breakfast before class. I'm starving.

"I'm not hungry," Sighed Alison.

"Well, I am."

Alison begrudgingly changed into sweatpants and a Tampa State sweater. The cafeteria was sparse, with only a few students eating a quick breakfast before their early morning classes. I got eggs and bacon while Alison got a big bowl of fruit loops with orange juice and a chocolate muffin.

"Low-carb dieter, I see."

Alison gave me a raspberry as she took a big swig of orange juice.

"Hey, we have a two game series this weekend against the Hurricanes. Why don't you come with me? It could be our little weekend getaway."

"What, go in a bus with a bunch of jocks?"

"Not exactly. But the girlfriends of some of the players car-pool during road games. It would be fun. Besides would be good for you to meet new people."

"I can't. I'm visiting my folks this weekend. I have relatives visiting from Michigan."

"The family thing, huh?"

"You could say that."

"Have you told your parents?"

"About what?"

"Us."

"No," Alison said, taking a bite of her muffin. The crumbs flaked and sprinkled onto her tray. "Mm, this is good. Want a bite?"

"When do you plan on telling them?"

She sighed, and wiped away the crumbs clinging to the side of her mouth." I don't know. I mean, I don't want to imply anything, you know? They never liked the idea of me going out with anyone while I'm in school. They gave me this whole speech about me not getting pregnant and that I should focus on my studies," she said with a roll of her eyes. "Besides, last year I got out of a two- year relationship. It took me a while to get over it. I don't want to rush into things."

"So, then what are we?" I asked.

"I don't know, I mean, we're just us, I guess."

"What does that mean?"

"Do we have to discuss this now, at breakfast?"

" When should we discuss it?" I pushed.

"Coop, I don't like you pressuring me into a relationship. Right now I like things the way they are."

"I would just like to know where we stand."

"Where we stand? Coop, we've been dating for a few months. You're taking this way too seriously."

I watched her finish her cereal and muffin without saying a word.

"I have to go, Coop."

"Can we can talk about this later?" I said grabbing her hand.

Her sigh made my skin crawl. "We'll see, okay? I'll call you."

Bryce never enjoyed practice. To him it was boring and pointless, except batting practice, where he could show off by hitting towering shots over the center field wall. The game was effortless for him, like water running down a stream. For us mere mortals, we had to work just to keep up. Coach Webb stood behind me as I threw bullpen. Zach had the radar gun. Webb would comment on my windup, offering advice after every pitch. He noticed I wasn't shoving off enough off the mound. Webb patted me on the shoulder whenever he didn't like a pitch, hovering over me as if his stint in the minor leagues made him the god of pitching coaches. During practice he would walk around the outfield and yell at players for screwing up a play. Dawson used him as a field general. It was stupid, but I never bothered to question Coach Dawson's methods. After warm-ups, Webb lectured me on the importance of focus. Visualizing the type of game you want to pitch, all down to how many strike outs you want. Sometimes he acted more like a self-help guru than he did a pitching coach.

I was on my third day's rest as I sat out our game against Miami. It was nice to get a day off. Zach ran over. "Did you hear?"

"Hear what?" I asked.

"The war. It started."

I jumped. "The invasion?"

"Yeah. It's all over TV."

I looked over to Miguel, who was stretching out in the outfield. I wondered if he meant what he'd said. If he was ready.

"Our little Miguel is going to war," Zach said.

"You seem excited for him."

"Not everyone gets to go to war. I sure as hell don't."

"Who does?"

"The crazy brave, that's who. Maybe Miguel is crazy brave after all."

Bryce went three for four in game two against Miami, hitting two home runs and four RBIs. After getting back into Tampa, we gathered around the large flat screens at the student commons in Orsini Hall, fixated on the images of explosions and flickers of light and smoke that engulfed downtown Baghdad. That world was far different from the quiet confines of Tampa State. We all stayed glued to the TV, watching the replays of smart bombs striking their targets. "It's really happening," Zach said.

Miguel watched intensely. Samson pressed Miguel about when he would get shipped off. "Soon, I hope," Miguel responded.

Bryce scoffed at the screen and turned it off.

"What the hell are you doing!?" Zach roared.

"You guys are so gullible," Bryce said.

"What are you talking about?" I said.

"Don't you see this war is all bullshit?"

"Bullshit? Are you nuts?"

"It's all fake. I told you, it's like that movie *Wag the Dog*. They could make all the crap up in some film studio."

"You must be taking Professor Walt's Modern Governments class.

That guy is a walking conspiracy theory. You should hear him on the Kennedy assassination," Zach said.

"I'm just a skeptic, that's all. Ah, what the hell do I know?"

"Nothing. That's for sure," Miguel said with a sneer.

"Hey, it ain't nothing against you, man. You got guts to go over there. Shit, none of us would go."

Samson got on the table and pretended to have a machine gun, sputtering machine gun fire with his mouth. "I would be a badass over there!" he yelled.

"Tough guy, huh?" I asked.

"Look who's talking, Mr. Eighty-Nine. This is coming from a guy who gets all sensitive because he can't hit the mark."

"Take that back," I said.

"Why should I?" Samson asked, jumped off the table and got within an inch of my face. I was about to shove him before Bryce stepped in-between us. "Don't you have anything better to do, like play with yourself?"

Samson clicked his tongue. "That comes later."

When Bryce and I returned to our dorms, I almost punched our dorm room wall before Bryce stopped me.

That's your throwing hand, genius."

"What the hell is Samson's deal?"

Bryce threw himself on the bed and crossed his feet and rested his head behind his hands. "The kid is a child. He knows he can get underneath your skin. That's why he does it. He can sense weakness. Don't pay any attention to him."

I clenched my fist and paced around the room. "You OK? Bryce said.

I didn't reply to him. I sat on the corner of my bed and cracked my knuckles.

"Earth to Coop. Are you OK?"

I stared back at Bryce and nodded. He scoffed and rolled over to take a nap as I stayed on the corner of my bed to watch him sleep.

Bryce and I liked going to the gym in the evening. There weren't as many students crowding around the weights, and it didn't hurt that the women's volleyball team practiced in the basketball court next to the weight room. Bryce spotted me while I bench pressed, leaving me with over two hundred pounds of weight on my chest as I struggled to lift the bar. "You gotta push through the pain, Coop. One more rep."

I pushed with all my strength, barely finishing the last rep. "You see. We all got that extra little something we never thought we had. That's how you're going to make it to the bigs."

"Why did you say that crap in front of Miguel?" I said after I finished my last rep.

"What are you talking about?"

"About the war. He could go over there."

"Oh relax, the guy isn't going anywhere. They'll send him to Hawaii or somewhere, polishing his ass in some office."

"How do you know?"

"What do you care?"

The question hung in the air, and I went for another set, finishing my workout with twenty minutes on a treadmill slick with leftover sweat. Afterwards Bryce had a date, so I stayed by myself in the dorm doing homework. I usually spent my Friday nights with Alison, but we hadn't spoken to each other for the past few days. I waited for her to call. I figured she was with her folks. *Or did I weird her out?*

Homework distracted me from my dissatisfied thoughts. As I was just about to turn the page of *Principles of Accounting*, Zach barged into the room, trumpeting to me and all of the inhabitants of Orsini Hall tonight's frat party, which, according to Zach, was the biggest of the year. Zach slammed my textbook shut, not even bothering to mark the page with my pencil.

"Accounting homework and Friday nights don't mix," Zach said.

I put away my books and changed into a pair of jeans and a white dress shirt. I spritzed some cologne my mom gave me for my birthday and brushed my teeth before Zach and I made our way to the fraternity part.

The Epsilon Zeta house was a few minutes' walk from the dorms The house was an institution of sorts, with its colonial style facade and southern charm. As the elder statesman of fraternity houses, it has played host to fraternity members as far back as 1923.

I doubted frat parties were much different back then. College was four years of the same alcohol-induced soiree with the same people who enjoyed nothing more than to drink themselves into oblivion.

Asking a college student not to drink is like asking them not to breathe. I watched as everyone made a fool out of themselves. That was far better a buzz than any drink could offer.

Zach stumbled towards me, two red plastic cups sloshing their contents all over the stained carpet. "Drink, will ya? You're embarrassing yourself."

"You can do all the drinking for me."

"What the hell did you even come for?"

"Not everything is about beer. Besides, I wanted the company."

"Why isn't Alison keeping you company?"

"It's complicated. I mean, she went to visit her folks," I took one of the half empty cups.

He grinned. "Beer tends to uncomplicate things."

"I thought it was the opposite," I commented.

The old wooden interior of the frat house consisted of dated, worn-out furniture that seemed to have never once been cleaned. There was a musty, library smell lingering around the revelry, a ghost of student parties gone by.

Bryce sat on couch with a brunette, each holding Styrofoam cups with some pink concoction that probably had enough alcohol in it to intoxicate the entire team. I wandered by myself in a sea of debauchery.

I was shocked when I saw her. Near the rickety old stairs Alison stood with a tall, brown-haired pledge. She was laughing and giggling while he spewed what I'm sure was utter stupidity just so that he could get in her pants. She didn't see me, fixated on her conversation with the frat boy.

Alison looked amazing. She was wearing makeup, something she never did for me. A red blouse hung on her shoulders, loose enough to reveal her cleavage and draped down low enough to expose her back. Her jeans hugged her curvy figure, and I stood motionless. Alison laughed again. The frat boy lead her up the stairs, with other frat boys hollering at the sight of one of their own taking a female to their second floor orgy. I watched them disappear into the upper quarters of the Epsilon Zeta house. I was about to follow them before Bryce caught my arm to introduce me to a new fraternity pledge who reeked of cigarette smoke and looked like he was ready to pass out.

I congratulated him before I walked to the edge of the stairs. I heard someone yell my name behind me, then felt an arm on my shoulder. I shoved it away, knocking over the beer Zach was holding.

"Whoa. What the hell?"

"Sorry. I thought you were someone else.

He studied my face.

"Bored?"

"I think I'm going home."

"What? The party just started."

"It's the same old party Zach," I said before darting out of the fraternity house.

"Where are you going? Zach yelled after me, but I escaped and wandered the confines of Tampa State, allowing my demons to eat me alive.

# Chapter 5

Saturday morning we had an inter-squad game. Some of us were still reeling from the previous night's party, which was a blur. After the game, I was supposed to tutor Bryce. I dreaded it. I despised the idea of teaching someone who had no interest being taught. The burden of being an intellectual in a baseball uniform.

I warmed up. Zach playfully smacked me in the ass mid-windup, and I threw a wild pitch that landed somewhere in the empty stands.

"You left early last night," Zach said.

"I did."

"You didn't miss much. The usual drunken circumstances."

"I'm sure," I said.

"What's eating you? Since last night you haven't been yourself."

"Nothing."

"Bullshit."

"I need to get focused."

"It's just an inter-squad game."

"Make sure you have the gun. I want you clocking me."

"Coach doesn't want you being clocked during a game. He thinks it's a distraction."

I looked right at Zach. "I don't give a shit what Coach thinks. Just clock me."

Zach was benched due to a tight shoulder. He sat in the dugout while Coach Dawson leaned over the steps on the opposite side of the diamond. It was a scoreless top of the first. I struck out Samson. That felt good.

"What did the gun say?" I asked after I ran back to the dugout.

"You had a hitless first," Zach replied.

Zach showed me the red digits that glared as if to mock me. Eighty-nine mph, it read in big bold red numbers. It was disgusting. The first inning ended. The mound felt good and firm. Warm up felt right. I threw hard, damn hard. *The gun must be wrong.* I dug my cleats in the dirt when Bryce approached home plate. A few practice cuts and he entered his stance. There was a slight smirk that emerged from his expression of effortless existence. To him this was just a game, but one with high stakes for everyone else. Perhaps life was a game to him. I thought games were supposed to be fun, but then I grew up.

"Play ball," the umpire yelled.

The catcher gave the sign. Fastball. I agreed. My fingers ran over the red stitching of the ball. My wind-up was smooth and frictionless. My nails dug deep into the leathery flesh of the baseball. I threw the pitch with all the strength I could muster. I exited my wind-up to watch the pitch travel to home plate as if it were in slow motion.

I remember little after that because everything happened so fast. All I could remember was how Bryce's face exploded. At least that's how Zach described it when my wild pitch hit Bryce in the face. The field was silent. The chatter, the hollering, the baseball talk that consumed the field transformed to an eerie silence.

Nobody moved. Just stood and watched. He lay on the ground in a puddle of his own blood. The dugouts cleared. Coach Dawson and some of the trainers surrounded Bryce, motionless on the red stained dirt. I couldn't get a clear view of his face. The rest of the team gathered around as my throwing hand trembled. The sound of an ambulance blared in the distance.

"Is he alright?" I asked Miguel.

"Looks bad man. His face is busted up."

I pushed through the throng of players. Most of Bryce's front teeth were blown out. His nose and right eye were severely bruised. It looked like his face was going to cave in. Blood was everywhere. He didn't seem conscious. "Bryce, can you hear me?" I asked. He didn't respond. His eyes danced behind his eyelids. Coach Dawson kept reassuring him. The trainers treated him before the medics arrived.

"Coop, help me lift him."

I, along with Coach Dawson and a trainer, lifted Bryce onto the stretcher. The medics rushed him off to the ambulance, driving to the nearest hospital. The game was over. Before I left the dugout, I saw the radar gun lying on its side on the blue chipped paint of the dugout bench, with ninety mph glaring back for me to see.

The waiting room smelled, like death and disinfectant. I sat alone while Zach, Coach Dawson, and a few others waited near the emergency room doors that swung like a gate to Purgatory. The smell kept reminding me of how awful it was to sit there. I was a heap of emotionless flesh while I waited for the news on Bryce's condition. Questions swirled in my mind. Would he be scarred for life? Would he play ball again? Would he even be the same? Could he die?

Most of the Silverback team waited in the lobby. Some of the players were crying while others stood motionless with stoic faces, like the ones you find in old black and white photos from the early 1900s. The team looked pretty shaken up. I wanted to be alone. I couldn't stand the crying and the grief. I wanted to just get up and leave, hoping no one would notice. I clenched the fist of my throwing hand hoping the throbbing pain would subside. I rubbed my hands together and took a deep breath to cool the adrenaline that wouldn't subside.

I was about to get up to buy a coke from the vending machine when Coach Dawson saw me sitting alone and rubbed my hair like a solemn father.

"You okay, Coop?" he asked.

"I suppose."

"It's not your fault. You know that? These things happen. The ball got away from you. That's all. It was a freak accident."

"Sure," I said.

" It happens. I was a hitting coach for the Yankees farm system. We had this new phenom, Taylor Raines on the mound. Kid had lights out stuff. I'm talking about a one hundred mile per hour fastball. He faced the leadoff hitter who hit a comebacker to the mound. Taylor didn't even have time to react. The line drive hit him squarely in the forehead. I can remember the sound the ball made when it hit his head. I don't have to tell you his career ended after that game. Hell, he's lucky he survived. But I'll never forget that sound. "

It was one of those things a ballplayer doesn't think will happen to them. But it does happen, that freak incident where lightning strikes and you get hit with a bean ball square in the face.

He did his best to reassure me. The other players did the same. I felt the weight of it on me like a sack of bricks. It seemed there was more sympathy for me than Bryce, and I was the one who hit him.

His mom rushed into the emergency room, yelling his name frantically while Coach Dawson held her back from rushing through the swinging doors of the operating room. I couldn't bare to look at her. I wondered if she knew I was the one who hit him. I watched as the other players gathered around, some getting hysterical like they were children. I gazed on like an outsider, trying to make sense out of what happened within the past few hours.

A doctor in scrubs walked through the doors. She spoke with her and Coach. They were stoic after the doctor spoke with them for ten minutes. I stood and marched to them to get some answers when I stopped myself, pacing back and forth, running my hands through my hair like I was ready to yank them out.

"You okay?" Zach asked tapping my shoulder.

"If only I got paid for how many times people asked me that."

"It's still a valid question, considering the circumstances."

"What's the word?" I asked.

"Doc said he'll be alright. But he will have get reconstructive surgery."

"Will he play ball again?"

"I think that's the least of his worries… Say, what happened out there?"

"What are you talking about? You were there."

"That's not what I meant," said Zach. "Since when have you ever hit anyone? I've never known you for throwing wild pitches."

"I don't think I like where you are going with this."

"Look, all I'm saying is…"He rubbed his hand over his forehead. "Forget it."

"Why don't you just come out and say it?"

"It's just. Maybe if you weren't so fixated on some damn number." He sighed. "I'm sorry. I'm just bent out of shape over it. That's all."

I got a Diet Coke from the vending machine and left Zach to ponder to himself. I had to get away from everyone. I sat in a chair in a barren hallway near a room with the door open. A nurse with a tray walked into it. I heard what sounded like gibberish coming from inside. I slid my chair so I could get a better look.

There was a patient with mopped brown hair and freckles and big brown eyes. He was a little younger than me. The nurse was trying to feed him but he kept slapping the fork away. "We all have souls but none of us had a say in it," he blurted out. His eyes danced around the room. Drool dribbled down his chin. The nurse took a napkin from the tray and cleaned his mouth when he looked in my direction. "Hi *strangeeer*," he said, looking straight at me as I wandered into the room.

The nurse noticed me staring. "Excuse me. Is there something I can help you with?" I remained fixated on the patient, whose stare seemed to look into my own madness.

"Sir. If you're not a relative, I'm going to have to ask you to leave."

The nurse marched to the door and closed it. I returned to the hospital lounge, the patient's glare still burned in my mind. I found Miguel sitting alone near a television displaying the latest news on the war.

"Where have you been?" he asked.

"Aren't you going to ask me if I'm okay?" I asked sarcastically.

"Well, yeah, are you?"

"Did I miss anything?"

"He's out of surgery. Most of the guys already came in to see him. Zach's in the cafeteria. I think I might go there myself. I haven't eaten all day."

The nurse escorted me to room 348. It had a nice view of the bay, similar to the one from our dorm. Bryce's mom and Coach Dawson were sitting by his bed. His face was bandaged up and swollen. Most of his teeth were missing. He was unrecognizable. "Coop." Mrs. Schwartz embraced me like I was her long lost son. She kissed me on the forehead. "I'm so sorry that this happened to both of you, Coop."

"I know you are. How's he doing?"

"He's alright, considering. They gave him some meds so he's sleeping. He might be up later."

"Where's Mr. Schwartz?"

"He had a convention to attend in Orlando. He should be in by this evening."

Mrs. Schwartz and Coach Dawson left to grab dinner in the cafeteria. I sat beside him. "Can you hear me?"

Bryce was in there somewhere. I wondered what he thought of me. I examined every inch of his bed. My attention returned to his face. *I did that*, I thought in disbelief. Bryce, a living, breathing example of imperfect perfection, who just yesterday seemed to be on top of the world, was now laid in a hospital bed clinging to dear life. I sat beside him. His chest moved up and down with every breath he struggled to take.

I felt like I did when I was on the field earlier that day. The adrenaline rushed through me like I was on the pitcher's mound. I glanced at the door to see if anyone was coming in. Bryce's heart monitor beeped with the rhythm of every thought that flashed through my mind. I recalled Miguel's story of the day his brother pushed him from that branch, the day he succumbed to darkness. "Can you hear me Bryce?"

I knew he couldn't, but I figured it would be worth a shot. I stood up and walked to the window. I stared out through the blinds of his room that overlooked the ocean. It was peaceful enough. But it didn't calm the anxiety buried within me.

I needed to tell Bryce somehow. To tell him the truth about what happened. I went back to his bed. Leaned over him. I stared into his swollen face. "I'm not sure why I did what I did today, Bryce. I'm not sure if you hate me or not. But I've been doing a lot of thinking about it. To tell you the truth, I'm not sure if I feel bad about it. Does that sound strange to you?"

The only response was his breathing and the heart monitor that kept beeping, telling me he was alive. I heard some footsteps outside the door, but when I looked I saw no one there. I went out into the hallway. It was empty, but I felt a presence. Like someone watching.

I sat in the chair in the corner of the room. I watched Bryce breathe. His stillness quieted my mind as I looked out again at the blue ocean.

It was late in the evening when Mr. Schwartz arrived. Mrs. Schwartz hugged him and returned to her seat as her husband looked over his son, touching the bandages on his face while he slept. I sat in the corner, hoping he wouldn't notice me, but I was foolish to think that. He turned to me like he had eyes in the back of his head. I stood from my chair and stuck out my hand for a shake. He took it and wrapped his arms around me.

"This isn't your fault, son." That was the theme of the evening. I nodded my head. "You look tired."

"A little."

"Why don't you go home? Get some sleep. He's not going anywhere."

"I might do that."

Mr. Schwartz pulled me aside into the hallway so that his wife wouldn't hear.

"I appreciate you staying here with Dana. She's a bit shaken up by all this. She doesn't understand the risks involved with playing this game, like we do. Listen, if you ever need to talk, I want to let you know I'm here."

I nodded as we awkwardly stared at each other, each waiting for the other to say something. He sighed and sat on a chair outside in the hallway. "I hate seeing him like that," He said.

"It's understandable," I replied, leaning against the wall.

He reached for a pack of cigarettes before he realized that smoking in a hospital wasn't the smartest idea, and shoved them back in his pocket. "Don't know how many times I've tried to quit," he said sheepishly.

"I remember when he was in little league." He smiled to himself. "Bryce was a chubby kid back then. He could barely fit into his uniform." I nodded, not quite able to picture the Bryce I know as 'chubby.

"You know, I appreciate you tutoring him. Bryce isn't always focused. I keep telling him he can't rely on baseball to make a living. You need to have something to fall back on. You're a good influence on him."

I nodded again, and watched a nurse with her hair rolled in a tight bun push a cart with food into the neighboring room.

"This is going to eat you up a bit, you know," Mr. Schwartz said.

"What?"

"Maybe not at first. But it's going to hit you. The guilt of it all. Resentment. You need to be prepared for that. You have to be a little crazy to be a pitcher. Sometimes your ego gets the best out of you. I know what it's like. When you're up there on that mound, it's not just you against the hitter. You're up there against yourself, and sometimes you might not like what you see," Mr. Schwartz said licking the end of his cigarette before sticking it back in its' carton.

"I'm fine, really, I am," I said.

"You don't have to act tough with me, son,"

"It's not about acting tough. I'll be fine. Worry about your son."

"And you don't think I am?" He snapped.

"I never said that."

Mr. Schwartz rubbed his hands on his face and stood. "Remember what I said. If you ever need to talk…."

"I'm. Fine."

He nodded and watched me leave.

Coach Dawson was the only one left from the team still at the hospital. He had dozed off in a chair in the lobby while waiting for me. We said nothing as we drove back to campus. I preferred it that way. There was nothing to say. I only hoped he would quit trying to make me feel better. I'd gotten enough of that for one day. The car rolled to a stop in front of Orsini Hall.

"Get a good night's sleep, Coop. And I want you to put what happened today behind you. Understand?"

I bid him goodbye, pretending to feel sorry for myself and that I needed time alone. The dorm was empty and quiet. I was accustomed to finding Bryce already passed out on his bed by this time. It still wasn't made, as usual.

I liked the quiet, the eeriness of it. Surprisingly, I wasn't tired. My arm felt great. I could have thrown bullpen if anyone had been up for it. Probably would've been in poor taste, considering Bryce's condition.

## Wild Pitch

I was too anxious to stay in my dorm. I raced to the closest dive bar I could find. I settled into a corner chair and ordered a beer, watching the ball game on the giant flat screen. I flicked leftover peanut shells with my finger while two men yelled at the flat screen because of an infield error. Cigar smoke drifted in between the lamplight hovering over the pool table with balls scattered throughout. The bar was small and cramped comprising of wooden bar tables and stools and a neon light for Budweiser flickering beside me.

I grabbed my beer. My finger circled the rim of the frosted mug while the TV blared in the background. An old man with a cane sat with his dog on the other side of the bar. The dome of his head shone in the dim light. He repeatedly pulled at his fraying sweater while blowing kisses at his dog, wagging his tail on the floor. He twiddled his thumbs and sighed before he took a sip of his beer, staring at the flatscreen with droopy eyes. The old man gazed at me from across the bar and nodded. I returned the nod and raised my glass and took a sip. He adjusted himself on his barstool, tucking in his disheveled sweater before his squinty little eyes met mine in my little corner of the world.

"Ball player? The old man called across the bar.

"What?"

"I've seen you at the games. I try to go to all the home games. Class of '67."

I rubbed my chin. "Thanks for coming to the games." He grabbed a treat from his pocket and tossed it in the dog's drooling mouth. "Hell of team you got this year."

I cracked my knuckles and fidgeted in my seat. "Yup."

"Must feel great to win all them games. When I was your age, I thought I was invincible. I was a ballplayer too you know. Played first base in high school. Hell your father probably wasn't even alive back then. Now look at me. I'm seventy-six damn years old. I got diabetes and arthritis. I gotta see seven damn doctors. Some of them I can't even pronounce their freaking names. I got one doctor telling me I have lay off red meat. Jesus H. Christ, I can't even piss anymore. I have to wear one of them damn diapers. Ah, hell, what are you gonna do? Don't get old kid," The old man laughed.

I nodded while staying glued to the Dodgers vs Giants game. It was tied in the second inning when I watched a pitch slam into the batter's knee. I became transfixed as the batter crumples like a rag doll and falls to the ground, a tense pause before he gets up and trots to first baseball. My clenched fists tremble against the glass, rattling it on the bar top. The bartender looks up from washing some dirty beer mugs next to me. "A little restless tonight?"

"I'm fine," I said, shaking my hands.

The old man got up and sat a seat closer. He pulled out a cigar from his pocket, ripped the tip of it off with his mouth and spit it out before he began to chew on it. "Boy, this last doctor I saw," he rambled, "What a pain in the ass. The one that doesn't want me eating read meat? He replaced Dr. Rogan. Had him for thirty damn years! Now I got this young punk telling me not to do this and not to do that."

Before he could say another word, I slammed my beer mug on the bar, sloshing some of it on my coaster.

"Does it look like I'm interested in talking to you?" I growled.

The old man flinched and glanced around the bar, his arm shaking while he grabbed his cane. "Why, I didn't mean nothing by it."

"This guy bothering you Alfonso?" The bartender said, wiping his hands with a towel while giving me a dirty look.

"I didn't mean nothing by it." The old man repeated.

The five dollar bill I tossed on the bar soaked up the beer I spilled. "I'm just trying to drink my beer in peace." I slid off my barstool and stalked towards the door. The damn dog yelped as my foot landed on its tail. I could hear the old man mutter under his breath, the bartender calming him down with another beer.

Once outside I inhaled the muggy night air. I was alone again, staring down a dark, lonely road, hesitant to cross it.

# Chapter 6

The campus was quiet on Sundays. Most students slept in or caught up on their schoolwork. I took a shower and changed into some jeans and a T-shirt when I heard a knock on the door. I was expecting one of the guys to pop in and check to see how I was doing, for which I had already prepared a generic reply.

"Alison?"

"Hi," she said. Alison looked great, even without makeup. I was surprised to see her.

"Come in."

She strolled around the room when I realized it was actually the first time she'd ever stepped foot in it. Alison smiled at the picture of Belushi hung on the wall. She stuffed her hands in her pockets as she looked around the room, tip toeing over some bundles of dirty clothes that lay on the floor before she stopped in front of my window.

"Nice view," she said.

"It is. Where have you been?" I asked.

"I was going to ask you the same thing."

"You never called."

"Am I the one who's always supposed to call?" she asked.

"I don't know. You seemed irritated after our last talk."

"I didn't come here to talk about that," Alison said crossing her arms.

"Oh."

"I heard about what happened yesterday."

The word spread quickly. I thought the school newspaper would have waited until Monday.

"I read about it online at the Gazette. Is he okay?"

"He'll need surgery."

"And what about you?"

The images of Alison walking up the stairs with that frat boy enraged me further. I felt inferior, like she was getting the best out of me. But I knew her secret. I wouldn't reveal this to her now. Oh, no. I was too distracted by the events of the previous twenty-four hours. The opportune time would come, I thought. I shrugged off her question like it was of little importance.

"When did you come back from your parents' house?"

Her cheek twitched, and she smiled as if I had just given her a compliment. "I got back on Sunday. I'm sorry I didn't call. My parents and I got into an argument. Their marriage is on the rocks and I'm usually the one trying to mediate every time they fight. I needed sometime to myself," she said, looking out over the Gulf.

"I see," I said.

"And you didn't answer my question."

"I'm fine."

"That's it. You're just fine?"

"These things happen, Alison. It was a freak accident."

"I suppose. He could have died."

"But he didn't," I spat.

She took an old baseball that sat on my night table and tossed it in the air. "Are we okay?"

"Why wouldn't we be?" I responded.

"Look, I know I'm difficult. But I do care for you. Even if I don't show it sometimes."

Alison kissed me and wrapped her arms around me. I wish it felt good. I really did.

Visiting Bryce became routine in the weeks that followed the incident. He went through several procedures, including some pricy dental work. The first two weeks Bryce was in and out of consciousness due to all the surgeries and meds. His parents were supportive of both of us. I appreciated that. My own parents seemed indifferent about my endeavors, and at times, my very existence.

Bryce was in recovery before another round of surgeries in the coming weeks. It was the first time I would have an actual conversation with him if that's what you could call it. There was a Rays game on when I entered. His teeth implants were still fresh. There were bandages and cuts on his face, but an improvement over when I'd last seen him. He kept watching the screen, unaware of my presence.

I tapped his shoulder. I thought he didn't recognize me at first. His features were still swollen but a smug grin surfaced through the bruised exterior. "Hey," he said groggily.

"How you doing?"

"Could be better," he said.

The nurse came in to check up on him. Another nurse entered with a tall styrofoam cup. "Still can't eat solid food yet," Bryce explained as he took a sip. The nurse fixed his pillow. His hair was uncombed.

"You must hate me." I said.

Bryce responded by raising the volume of the television, grimacing when he turned his head.

"I don't hate you. You could have been more careful," He sighed and moaned when he adjusted himself on the bed. "You are an asshole though."

"Yeah. Right." I said.

"This will change things," Bryce said.

I raised my voice and leaned towards the bed. "How?"

"How am I going to get drafted? Teams don't want a cripple."

"That's the meds talking. You need to rest."

"I've rested enough," Bryce said staring at the TV. "Have any of the guys visited?"

"Not lately. Look, I have to tell you something." I got up and shut the television off.

"The game isn't over." Bryce was becoming drowsier with each passing minute as I raced to tell him what was buried deep inside me. The pain meds taking their effect.

"This is more important."

"I'm getting tired. Maybe later."

"This can't wait."

He became drowsy and fell asleep. I got the nurse. "What's wrong with him?" I asked hurriedly.

"He needs his rest. He'll sleep for a few hours."

"Can you wake him up? I need to tell him something."

"Young man, I'm not going to wake him. He needs his rest. You can come by later if you like. His parents will be here by then," the nurse said adjusting his pillow.

I left him alone with the nurse and headed back to campus. In my dorm, alone, I heard a knock. Expecting Alison, instead I found Zach.

"Where were you?" he asked.

"I went to see Bryce."

"How is he?"

"Somewhat conscious," I replied. "I haven't seen any of the guys at the hospital."

"Ball players don't need to be reminded of their own mortality."

"That's your excuse?" I said.

"It's not an excuse. Just superstition," Zach said.

Baseball players are a superstitious bunch, from eating waffles every morning before a game to using the same cup. It's the routine we think will make us the next Derek Jeter. A path to greatness.

"Wanna go down to O'Brien's? Miguel's leaving tomorrow. We should send him off the right way."

"Sure. You mind if Alison tags along?"

"The more the merrier."

O'Brien's was no cleaner than a toilet seat, with a residue that covered the floors that made the soles of your shoes stick to it like a wet puckered kiss. Alison thought it was quaint. The hospital smelled better. But the beer was cheap and the company free. Alison gripped my hand underneath the table as Miguel, Samson, and Zach did shots.

"You won't have a shot?" Alison asked.

"I have more refined taste in alcohol."

"I forgot." she said.

After several shots Miguel was still sober, arguing that the bartender gypped us with watered down drinks. It was probably true.

"When do you ship out?" I asked Miguel.

"O' five hundred tomorrow morning. Heading for officer's training in Georgia. Then off to Germany."

"Then Iraq?"

"Probably."

Zach raised a toast to Miguel. Our glasses chimed as we sent Miguel off into the real world, away from the safe confines of Tampa State. Miguel left us shortly after that.

"Going to war sucks," Zach said.

"Miguel doesn't think so," I responded.

"How do you know?" Zach asked.

Samson did his best to hit on Alison. She had none of it, getting Samson agitated over her rejection.

"Where did you find this girl?" asked Samson.

He picked up on it and waved his finger at me. One mph. I

shoved his finger away. After another drink, we left Zach and Samson to drink to their hearts' content.

Awhile later, I stared at the gyrating ceiling fan, as Alison and me lay in bed together in my dorm. I heard her say something, but I was fixated staring at the gyrating ceiling fan entering a self-induced trance.

"Hello!" Alison said waving her hand in front of my eyes.

"Sorry."

She scoffed and rolled over with her back facing me.

"You've been acting weird tonight. You didn't even last long."

"I'm tired. That's all."

Alison wrapped her arms around my waist.

"Is it about what happened?"

"I don't want to talk about it."

"There's obviously something wrong."

"What makes you think that?"

"You seem distant. Like, I don't know, you're not telling me something."

"I suppose we all have secrets, Alison."

"Secrets?"

"It's just an observation. That's all."

"I wouldn't hide anything from you."

I wanted to laugh or scream. She thought her little secret was safe and secure. I knew mine was. It felt like a warm blanket of anonymity that camouflaged my lies. She seduced me again, and at that moment, that's all that mattered.

The season was winding down. I lost my last three starts. Bryce left the hospital and stayed with his parents. None of us heard much from him, other than that he was alive. I pressed my arm to its limits.

# Wild Pitch

A part of me didn't want us to make the playoffs, not that it was likely considering we were barely hovering over five hundred. I was tired and worn out and in desperate need of rest. I felt a burden on my shoulders. Not so much from the season, but from what I'd done. It felt like an anchor in my stomach dragging me down to where I couldn't stand being in my own skin.

It was a hot one against Florida Atlantic. The sun's heat stretched across the field, casting a layer of haze that burnt your skin when you stepped onto the field. Jay Zysk was the new catcher, a twenty year old with a good arm but a better bat.

He liked to pull the ball. Coach wanted him to spread the ball throughout the field. Jay liked the long ball, but what ball player didn't? I fanned the first three batters, despite Jay and I miscommunicating with the signals. He didn't understand me like Bryce did. I ragged on him pretty good to the point where Zach had to separate us.

"Easy on the kid, huh? Besides, you struck out three."

"If he keeps getting the signals mixed up that won't always be the case."

Samson hit a solo shot to put us up one nothing. My arm was giving me trouble in the top of the second. There was pain around my rotator cuff. The Florida Atlantic left fielder approached the batter's box, digging deep into the dirt to entrench himself for battle.

Jay gave the sign. Fastball inside. He was starting to get it. I got in my wind-up and felt a pinch in my arm when I released the ball. The fastball travelled off course, sailing above the head of the batter. Other times it would have been shrugged off as a bad pitch. But in this case, I could hear the dugouts gasp as the pitch flew above the batter's helmet, which he threw to the ground as he charged the mound.

He shoved Jay aside like he was a rag doll. I braced for impact. He took a swing at me, which I dodged. His second punch, however, landed square in my jaw. The dugouts cleared. Zach picked me up off the grass.

The commotion lasted for a few minutes before the umps got things under control. Several players from the Silverbacks and Florida

Atlantic had to keep the left fielder from ripping my head off as I was escorted off the field.

Word had got out about what I'd done to Bryce. I was beginning to get a reputation as a headhunter. I was tossed from the game. The docs took an MRI of my shoulder. Tendinitis. Nothing serious. But we failed to make the playoffs and Coach Dawson decided to shut me down for the rest of the season, which gave me more time to dwell on my demons.

# Chapter 7

With my season over, I also had more time to spend with Alison. She liked the beach, one of the perks of living in Florida. After our last day of class we went to Clearwater, staying at this small, cheap hotel with a great ocean view. The walks on the beach were as cliché as they came, but who says clichés are a bad thing? I forgot about Bryce. I hadn't heard from him in several months. Alison's secret, at least for the moment, was an afterthought.

Summer wasn't long enough. The days went by as fast as the ocean breeze that swept Alison's hair whilst we both cuddled on the hotel balcony, admiring the sunset. As I said, clichés don't have to be a bad thing.

We spent most of the time taking road trips and staying with friends who had an extra bed to spare. It was early August when Alison went to visit a friend of hers in Tallahassee. I decided it was time to see my folks at least once before the summer ended.

The visit with my parents was unspectacular, asking generic questions about school and my social life. They wanted to know how Bryce was doing. I told them I hadn't heard from him. They weren't surprised, nor did they show the least bit of interest in any aspect of my life, other than verifying that the small amount of money they spent on my tuition was well earned. My father, Bill, was a meticulous accountant, and probably the most frugal son of a bitch in the state of Florida. Everything to him was about the numbers. Majoring in Accounting wasn't much of a choice. It was the only way my parents would pay for school since my father thought most degrees were absolutely worthless. Though sophomore year, I earned an athletic scholarship, pleasing my father, the only thing he appreciated in me playing baseball. My mother cared about me when it suited her, but she had her own secrets. She despised my father.

My parents grew up in New Jersey. They met while attending Montclair State and got married shortly after graduation. Dad started working for Cain and Swanson, a small accounting firm in New York. But the high taxes and the commute from Jersey inspired him to make the move to Florida, where there was no state income tax and cheaper lifestyle.

Mom didn't want to move. But my father was as stubborn a man as I've ever met. They moved anyway, leaving most of her family behind. Mom became a shadow of her former self. She was a beautiful woman. A prom queen and a cheerleader who could've gotten any man she wanted. Yet, she somehow ended up with an accountant whose idea of fun was catching a movie and be in bed by ten. My mother had thought he was endearing. Perhaps pity had something to do with it. She was a sentimentalist and revered the past, fawning over her glory days.

"Are you dating anybody right now?" she asked as she washed the dishes after dinner.

"Yes."

"What's her name?"

"Alison."

"That's a nice name. Is it serious?"

"I think it's getting to that point."

"Oh," She said in a voice that wouldn't crack a decibel. She sat on the kitchen counter and lit up a cigarette, which she only did when my father was out of the house.

It was one of the few things she enjoyed. The smoke curled up around her black hair, still wavy and well made. She used just enough makeup to accentuate her hazel eyes while masking the wrinkles that showed her age.

"How long have you two been dating?"

"Since last summer."

"Is she a nice girl?"

"Yes. Interesting, but nice."

"Good."

"How are things between you and Dad?"

"They are what they are," She said crossing her legs taking a long drag.

She grinned with every drag of the cigarette. I couldn't for the life of me understand why she never divorced my father. Maybe despite her resentment towards him she still somehow loved him. Perhaps it was the convenience. Divorce is a nasty, messy enterprise.

The smoke from the cigarette drifted out through the open window, clearing away any evidence from my father, who still thought she'd quit smoking ten years earlier. Another secret. Some of us have more than others. I speculated what others my mother might have. Maybe there was another man.

I decided not to wait until my father got back. I said goodbye to her. She put out the cigarette in an ashtray she still kept hidden in her armorer. "Why don't you wait for your father?"

"I want to get settled in before the semester starts."

Her embrace was lukewarm as if we were strangers who were saying goodbye after a brief chat.

"Stay in touch."

"I will," I said.

She watched me from the kitchen window as I drove away.

The Tampa State Campus was bustling with activity. Orientation and campus tours zipped around with groups made up of parents and wide-eyed college freshmen.

The dorm was musty and hot. Bryce's belongings were gone, except for the bed sheets, which were tucked and wrapped neatly. Nobody knew when he was coming back. Not even Coach Dawson.

The view of the Gulf was just as nice as when I'd left it the previous semester. That brought a smile to my face. I heard a knock on my door.

"Welcome back," Zach said, holding an envelope.

Zach spent the summer playing city ball, which he likened to a glorified little league of a bunch of ragtag misfits who still wanted to play organized baseball.

"It's like the Bad News Bears all over again," Zach said.

"At least you played," I replied.

"How's the arm?"

"Better. I got the all clear from the doc last week. Should be ready to go."

"Good. By the way, I got your mail. I didn't open it. It looks like a letter. Who the hell sends letters anymore?"

"There are still some traditionalist left in this world. Who is it from?"

"Miguel."

"Miguel?"

"It's from his home address. I thought he was already overseas?"

"So did I."

I opened the envelope to find a letter written on plain loose-leaf paper. It felt personal and intimate.

*Coop;*

*I hope all is well. I just got back from Iraq. It's important you see me.*

*Miguel*

I shredded the letter and threw the strips of paper in the garbage. "What did you do that for?" What did it say?"

"Nothing that concerns you, Zach."

"Miguel is my friend too."

"But he wrote to me, not you."

"Oh, that makes you special. Let me read it!"

Zach kept pressing me but I didn't budge. I understood what it meant to keep a secret. Zach gave up and mumbled a few obscenities before returning to his dorm room.

Miguel's home was in Riverview, about a 45-minute drive from the university. The town sat near a power plant, its' smoke stack billowing white, thick fumes amid the open pastures and fields making up the surrounding area. I parked on the side of a dirt road and walked up to a ranch-style home with chipped yellow paint and a broken screen door. The lawn looked like it hadn't been mowed in weeks. Miguel's red 89 Supra was sat in the driveway beside a late nineties Ford Explorer. I rang the bell. The door opened. From Mrs. Fuentes' scrunched facial expression, I could see that she was not happy to receive visitors. "Hi. My name is Coop. I'm here to see Miguel."

"Why?" she asked.

"I played ball with him at school."

"Mom, it's alright," Miguel yelled from the back of the house.

"Come in," Mrs. Fuentes said returning to a stack of papers and a calculator. "You want something to drink?"

"No thanks, Mrs. Fuentes."

"Miguel just finished taking a shower. He'll be out in a moment."

She pinched the bridge of her nose in sheer frustration as she returned to looking over her documents. "You wouldn't know anything about taxes, would you?"

"I am an Accounting major." That brightened her mood, but quickly faded when I told her I wouldn't be much help. She had filed an extension and was having problems writing off some expenses for her failing consultation business, which, ironically enough, focused on helping small and underdeveloped businesses.

Miguel emerged from the hallway nextto the kitchen. He had a five o'clock shadow and his hair looked like it hadn't been cut for some time.

"Glad you could make it, Coop, come on back" Miguel said.

I followed him to his bedroom. A relic from his past. He had some *Star Wars* figurines still in their boxes on his bookshelf. "Are you on leave?"

"No," he said. His officer's uniform hung in a hanger in his open closet, neatly pressed. He stared out the window from the corner of his bed.

"I got back from Iraq several months ago."

He had this thousand-yard stare. He had seen things. Things that would haunt most men. He wasn't the same Miguel I knew when he was one of us. His eyes danced around room in a paranoid frenzy. When he spoke he would look the other direction hoping not to make eye contact. There were bags under his eyes. He smelled of body odor and his bed a mess with clothes and trash littered on top of it.

He kept staring at the wall between sentences. I had to tap him on the shoulder to get his attention.

"Are you OK? What happened over there?"

There was an awkward pause. Miguel wrapped his arms around himself hoping that would stop him from trembling. He tried to say something but he just shook his head gave out a nervous laugh. "Why don't we get some fresh air,"" I insisted.

Miguel and I went for a walk in a park near his house. There were a few trees and thick green grass, like the grass at Brass Field, only thicker. There was something about Miguel that was off. That boyish enthusiasm for the greater good had vanished along with a foundation for sanity. He repeated questions over and over again as if he'd forgotten he'd already asked them. "How's Bryce?" he asked.

"I already told you, Miguel," I said, irritated.

"I read about it in the Silverbacks Gazette. Sucks you guys didn't make the playoffs."

"Right," I said shaking my head in frustration.

We sat by a tree no different than the one Miguel and I sat by back at campus. He picked off chunks of bark from the tree and drew shapes in the dirt, laughing as he did.

"Are you alright?"

"Are you?" he asked.

There was something about that moment that compelled me to tell him the truth about what I did to Bryce and why. It felt right to tell him. When I did, he didn't seem surprised. But it was when he turned to look at me my heart raced. My breath left my lungs while I contemplated if this was his madness consuming him. His eyes grew, and his grin went wide like a clown who was about to play a joke.

"… Savage."

He was about to laugh when I lunged at him. We wrestled on the ground for a moment before I was on top of him, putting all my weight on his chest. I pulled his shirt to get his face close to mine, screaming at the top of my lungs. I wanted to punch him. I raised my fist. It shook as I held my fist in the air. I punched the grass beside his right ear and lifted myself off of him. Miguel stayed on the grass for a while.

"Does he know?" Miguel asked.

"Shut up!" I yelled

I extended my hand and lifted him off the ground. He was still catching his breath when we made it back to the house. His mom was making dinner.

"What happened to you two?" Mrs. Fuentes had noticed the dirt and grass on our clothes.

"Nothing," Miguel said.

Her glower towards me was all too obvious. "What do you mean, nothing happened?"

"Is dinner ready?" Miguel said scratching his chin.

Mrs. Fuentes pressed both of us, but Miguel and I played dumb. She was hesitant, but invited me for dinner. She made lasagna with garlic bread and a salad with thick sliced tomatoes on top of the greens. The lasagna was good. It was homemade. None of that TV dinner crap my mom used to make. I finished my first plate and got seconds. Miguel was barely touching his.

"You should eat, honey," Mrs. Fuentes implored.

"I'm already full."

"But you barely touched your food."

Miguel stared at his food most of the time; occasionally looking up at me with a grin, ready to burst into laughter.

Mrs. Fuentes turned to me. "How long have you known Miguel, Cooper?"

"Since I was a freshman," I said.

"That's strange. Miguel never told me about you."

Miguel's chuckling was hysterical and demented.

"What's the matter with you, Miguel?" his mom asked, concerned.

"Such a savage, Coop. You don't play nice."

Tears dripped down Mrs. Fuente's cheeks as Miguel rambled on, speaking utter nonsense. I helped Mrs. Fuentes with the dishes. She insisted I sit down and stay for dessert, wiping away the tears rolling down her cheeks. Miguel composed himself for the moment, scarfing down chocolate ice cream in a green bowl. I saw her observe Miguel from behind the dinner table as he ate his dessert. Her boy was not the boy she'd raised. He'd changed. Something set him off. He was like a time bomb that was armed, *tick tock tick tock*. I sympathized with the thought. Maybe we were all ticking time bombs, set off by the right combination of events that had transpired by sheer luck or by our own doing.

Mrs. Fuentes retired to the bedroom, slamming the door. Miguel wanted to walk me to my car, but I declined and left. He stood behind the screen door, laughing as I drove away.

# Chapter 8

The semester was about to begin, and the campus was alive and rich with youth. I was now a senior, my last year of college before I would enter the real world. None of us were sure where we would end up after graduation. Some might make the pros, but that was always a long shot. If the majors didn't work out, I had an 'exciting' career as an accountant waiting for me. I still had told no one about Miguel. It was pointless.

I went for a run through campus, dodging and weaving between the swarms of students that bustled through the inner workings of Tampa State. I stopped by the dock and admired the ocean view. I watched a small fishing boat bob up and down on the water's surface, as the fisherman prepared to set off hoping to catch something worthwhile. Perspiration dripped down my back. I felt the adrenaline, a dose of freedom I hadn't felt in a long time. For the moment, secrets didn't matter.

I rushed up the three flights of stairs in Orsini Hall and ran down the hallway to my dorm, my heart pumping to the very end. When I opened the door, I found myself staring at the soles of a pair of sneakers that stuck out from the edge of the bed, an ESPN magazine obscuring the view of the bed's occupant.

"What are you doing?" I asked sternly, thinking it was some dumb freshman who'd gotten the wrong room.

"Is that how you treat an old pal?" The magazine came down, revealing Bryce's face.

"You're back?"

"I sure am, buddy. Literally just walked through the door ten minutes before you strutted in."

"Your face. It… Well… It looks great."

"Nothing a little plastic surgery can't fix." Bryce showed off his new teeth implants, as white as the pillow his head lay on. "These new chompers cost ten grand. Nice, huh?" There was a slight scar close to his left eye. His face chiseled from the plastic surgery. Still a huge improvement from the day I stood over him at home plate and watched the blood ooze out of it.

"Why didn't you call? You could have told me you were coming."

"I preferred to surprise all you fruitcakes."

My throwing hand trembled trying to untie the laces of my sneakers. No matter how much I tried to stretch out my fingers, I couldn't stop my hand from shaking. I finally ripped off my sneakers off and threw them to the corner of the room.

"Aren't you happy to see me?"

"Sure. I mean, yes, of course. It's just, well…."

Bryce took me by the shoulder and in a sympathetic manner said. "There aren't any hard feelings, Coop. Things happen. It was a freak accident. You got nothing to feel guilty for. I just want to let you know you're still my best friend. I'm your catcher. That won't change."

I slid Bryce's hands off my shoulders. "Do you remember when we saw each other at the hospital? What we talked about?"

Bryce thought for a moment, cracking his jaw. "No, not really. I mean, I was drugged up most of the time. Hell, I don't remember what I had for breakfast yesterday," he joked.

"There's something I gotta tell you, Bryce."

"What?"

My speech halted as I attempted to smoke out what had been aching inside me all this time. I was angry at Bryce. His return reminded me of my own provocations. A sense of dread consumed me as shackles of pain tightened around my mind.

The dorm room burst open. Zach lunged at Bryce, tackling him on the bed, followed by uproarious laughter. "Good Lord, I thought you were dead!" Zach said.

"Seriously?" Bryce asked.

"Nah, but you've been under the radar for months. We were all worried about you, kid. Didn't think you were coming back."

"I'm sorry to disappoint you, but not only am I back, I got the all clear to play this coming season. I'll get to catch this bum again," Bryce replied, leaning off the bed to smack my backside.

"We have to celebrate! Round up the usual suspects."

The Texas Bull was a rodeo-themed bar forty-five minutes away from campus with cheap beer and enough line dancing to satisfy any yearning for southern comfort. After a few beers, Samson jumped on the mechanical bull. It gyrated violently, throwing him off after only a few seconds. Alison coughed up her drink laughing at the spectacle.

"Why ride a bull when you can ride a ball player?" he yelled at a bachelorette party, amongst which the soon-to-be bride adjusted her wedding veil as she waited her turn to mount the mechanized beast.

"Where the hell is Miguel?" Bryce asked. "Has he talked to anyone?"

"Ask Coop. He saw him last," Zach said.

"You did? He's back?" Bryce asked.

"I thought he was in Iraq by now?" Samson said.

"He was."

"What do you mean?" asked Bryce.

"Miguel came back."

"He did? What did he say?"

I told them there wasn't much to tell, other than Miguel seemed off after returning from Iraq. The war had changed him. It was a real education, with no way of knowing if you passed or not. Bryce's demeanor changed from jubilation to disbelief at the hard reality of Miguel's transformation, and the ways of the real world that awaited him when college was over. He sipped his beer and watched the bride-to-be last longer than Samson had on the mechanical bull.

"She's lucky." Samson said.

Alison and I played pool. She beat me two out of three. "Wanna play for money?" she joked.

"You'll clean me out," I said spinning the eight ball on the table, ignoring a server who asked me if I wanted a drink.

"You okay?" she asked.

"Sure."

"Is it about Miguel?"

"Just thinking. It's our last year," I said.

"You think too much," Alison said.

She kissed and hugged me for a bit.

"You coming over tonight?"

"I can't. Bryce and me have some catching up to do."

"Oh, okay." She nodded and bit her lip.

"You don't approve?"

"No, it's fine."

"I need to talk with him about something. It's important."

"What is it you have to tell him?"

"It doesn't concern you," I said while trying to hide my trembling hand.

"Why?"

"Because I don't want you involved."

"You're not making any sense, Cooper."

"Can we drop it?"

"Why do you always do this?"

"Do what?"

"I feel like I'm just scratching the surface with you. Like there's a different person in there. I can never read you."

I grabbed her hand and squeezed it. "Look who's thinking too much now."

I dropped Alison back off at her dorm. The rest of us went bar hopping, carousing through Ybor City, a leftover of the once-vibrant Tampa cigar industry. Seventh Avenue comprising of two storey buildings dating back to the beginning of the 19th century, with balconies, wrought iron benches, and globe street lamps decorating the vibrant street. Ybor, a smaller version of New Orleans, offered the only real nightlife that suited us.

The characters of Ybor danced and paraded up and down the city streets, each bar as an oasis of intoxication. I enjoyed the people watching. There wasn't anything better than observing other people make a complete fool of themselves. Bryce was drunk, obnoxiously drunk. It annoyed me, how drunk he was, because I would end up having to take care of him. We had breakfast at a nearby diner and stumbled back to campus at three a.m. I helped him stumble up the stairs and laid him on his bed, falling asleep.

I thought about calling Alison, but it was late and she was asleep – or was she? My mind raced. Maybe she's with the frat boy. Things had been better without Bryce. Why did he have to come back? I knew his return was inevitable, but I suppose it was just wishful thinking that he would disappear into obscurity.

I went for a walk alone.

Campus was eerily quiet, yet serene. I had it all to myself, to explore its labyrinth of sidewalks and inner workings as much as I pleased, and no one else would know about it. The window in Alison's dorm room was dark. I stood and watched waiting to see if the light would flicker on.

Brass Field was in hibernation, waiting for the awakening of a new spring. Life seemed to matter more during the season. Playing baseball was better than sobriety. Without Bryce, it was manageable. With him back though, a burden returned that made the anticipation of the season almost unbearable.

Secrets took the main stage again. My knowledge of Alison's secret encouraged a deep internal rage, my own secrets that refused to stay dormant. I observed my dorm from afar, interpreting the feelings that were getting the better of me. There was only one logical conclusion I could draw from all this. It was the only one that made any sense. Coming to such a realization was awesome; yet, it made me question my own morality and who I was. But one thing was clear, and it was this. I hated Bryce Schwartz. I hated him with every ounce of my being.

# Chapter 9

Patrick Buckhorn, a man in his early forties with a strong athletic and business pedigree, relished the role as Tampa State's new Athletic Director. Since the university's privatization in the early nineties, the impoverished athletic program struggled to keep up with its well-funded competition., The fledgling program relied heavily on private donations and meager proceeds from tuition. We didn't even have a football team. To a former All American football star like Patrick Buckhorn, this was nothing short of humiliating.

After ten long years in investment banking, his inner athlete itched to compete again, to recall his glory days of Notre Dame and the New York Giants. He saw a challenge in Tampa State's program, and an opportunity. We were known for baseball and lacrosse, but after not winning a championship for the last five years, the university president, Jane Marquis, and the rest of the school's administrators were desperate to bring in someone to change all that.

A week before the season started, Buckhorn met with Coach Dawson, Bryce, and me for lunch at the Pelican, a buffet-style restaurant on the fifth floor of the Greco Center. It was my first time there since it's luxury dining wasn't part of my food plan.

The food looked appetizing enough. Stuffed chicken breasts

and tortellini steamed under hot lights. Buckhorn was dressed in a crisp, pressed grey Brooks Brothers suit, every inch the money maker, especially sitting next to Bryce and me in our jeans and rumpled dress shirts with our sleeves rolled up. Coach Dawson was always business casual when he was out of uniform.

Buckhorn was the only one with an empty plate and a cup of black coffee. He talked a good game. He was warm, friendly, and inviting, with a keen ability to dissect any conversation he was engaged in. Our conversation flowed easily, and we chatted about everything from baseball and academics to when he caught a pass from Eli Manning. When you spoke, he looked directly at you, absorbing every word that reached his ears. Buckhorn asked about the team and our expectations for the coming season.

"They're good, Patrick. We have a few freshmen I think could be starters right now. We got a good blend of underclassmen and seniors that can make us competitive." Dawson said.

"Competitive?" asked Buckhorn. Coach had difficulty elaborating. Buckhorn was visibly frustrated by the vagueness of Dawson's answer. He wanted clarity, not generalities.

"I'm sorry if I'm putting you on the spot, Coach, but 'competitive' could mean a lot of things. What I want to know is do we have a championship team?"

"Yes, we do. That's why I brought Bryce and Cooper here. These are my best players. I planned on waiting to announce it until after our meeting, but I decided to make Bryce team captain and Cooper co-captain."

A sudden jolt of shock raced through my entire body. I wasn't sure if they noticed my face turn red. Or my eyes exploding with anger. Even with my promotion, I was in Bryce's shadow. Co-captain was an insult. Coach might as well have spit in my face.

When I reached for the glass of water, I knocked over the glass and spilled its contents all over the table. Buckhorn grabbed several napkins and draped them over the mess, all with a smile.

Bryce was quick to return to the subject at hand. "Let me say something, Coach. Coop here is one of the best pitchers this school's ever had. With my help, I'm going to make him the best this school's ever had. With his arm, we're certain to win a championship."

I wanted to strangle Bryce. Coach Dawson gave him a scornful look as he babbled away; promoting himself even better than Buckhorn promoted Tampa State Athletics. All Buckhorn did was nod his head.

"You seem pretty confident," Buckhorn said.

"You gotta have confidence to play baseball, Pat." Buckhorn eyes squinted at the informality. He turned to me.

"What do you think, Coop? Can deliver us a championship?"

"I think so, sir."

"Think?"

"I suppose I'm just being modest."

Buckhorn winked. "Sure you are."

Buckhorn laid out his vision for Tampa State Athletics. I could tell the guy liked hearing himself talk. He'd been through enough boardroom meetings, spearheading multi-million dollars deals, to know how to come to an agreement. First it was to renovate James Brass Field. The bleachers were falling apart, and the field had poor irrigation, causing it to flood with just the slightest amount of rain. Buckhorn talked football, hoping to bring a team in the next six years. He visualized a state-of-the-art sports complex, with advanced training equipment and facilities to help foster a new era for TS Athletics. But all of this would need some serious funding.

"Gentlemen, I don't have to remind you that donors want winners. There's only so much I could do to raise capital. That's where you come in. You hold the future of Tampa State's athletic program in your hands."

"How much money are we talking about here?" I asked.

"For the new sports complex, sixty million, and that includes the football stadium. But the figures can change. They always do."

"So if we win, we get a piece of those donations?" Bryce said.

"Jesus, Bryce," I whispered to myself.

Buckhorn smiled. "I think we know the answer to that, Bryce. But you two can leave a strong legacy here for future generations of Tampa State Athletes."

"For sure," Bryce said.

"Tell me, what are your plans after graduation?" Buckhorn asked the two of us.

"Both of them have been scouted by some pro teams. But I always emphasize the importance of education." Coach Dawson said.

"I believe I was asking them, Mr. Dawson," Buckhorn said smugly.

Bryce talked about going pro. He was offered a few minor league deals but his dad wanted him to finish school before he signed. Plus some teams wanted to see how he would do in his senior year after his injury. Bryce was upbeat, selling himself to Buckhorn.

"Maybe the pros. I've talked to a few scouts. I'm majoring in Accounting, and I might go work for a top five firm," I said.

"Good for you," said Buckhorn. "You can do a lot with an Accounting degree."

"Sure"

Buckhorn paid the bill and thanked us for joining him, leaving us for a meeting.

"Sweet, free lunch," Bryce said.

"Coach, can I talk to you a minute, alone?" I asked.

Bryce got a third helping from the buffet while Coach Dawson and me spoke outside the entrance of The Pelican.

"Coach, I wish you would have told me and the rest of the team before making Bryce and me captains. I thought you hated the idea."

"Things have changed, Coop. We have a chance at a winner this year. The team respects both of you." Coach put his arm around my shoulders. "Look, you're a leader on this team. You handled yourself well after what happened last year. Most guys would've gotten shaken up and quit. You hung tough. You're a good pitcher, Coop, and I need your *A* game this year. A lot is riding on this season. With your help we have a real shot."

I nodded while Coach smiled and left for a meeting.

Bryce finished his third serving and met me outside The Pelican.

"Captains. Who would've thought?" Bryce shook his head. "We're big time now."

I fumed at his cavalier grin. "What the hell was that all about?"

"Huh?"

"Trying to play me up like that?"

"Oh, would you relax? It's called marketing, buddy. Haven't you learned anything in business school?"

"Christ, Bryce, I don't need this pressure."

"Sometimes a little pressure is good for you. Keeps you motivated. Trust me. I did you a favor. The guy likes us."

"Favor? I don't think using me to make yourself look good in front of the Athletic Director is a favor."

"What are you talking about?"

I squeezed my fist till it turned red. "Forget it," I said.

It was evening, but the sun continued to cast an amber glow over the campus. We came back to the softball field just like before. Bryce was suffering from cramps after a heavy weight-lifting session. He squatted four hundred pounds, a little much even for a guy his size. He managed one rep and slammed the barbell on the squat rack, letting out a loud primal grunt to alert the rest of the gym rats of his conquest.

There was no radar gun. No distractions. Just Bryce and me on the field. I wished we could use Brass Field. Damn Coach and his paranoia. We would have made sure the field was well kept. My arm felt loose and good as the ball jumped off my hand with authority. The sound of the ball popped Bryce's mitt, echoing in the space around us. It was the most right thing I have felt in a while. It made sense. There were no illusions with pitching. It was just the catcher, the batter, and me.

The lights of the field kicked on. A few girls from the women's softball team practiced in the outfield. They didn't seem to mind our intrusion on their turf. Bryce distracted by a blonde wearing tiny spandex shorts, rifling balls from one end of the outfield to the other. "Whoa, she's got an arm." Bryce lifted up his mask and stood up to get a better look.

"Oh, I'm sure you like her because of her arm," I said.

"Hey, I've always appreciated a woman with a good arm. Okay?"

"Bullshit," I said.

"Why don't we call it a day? My legs are killing me. I can barely walk."

"You shouldn't squat so much," I remarked.

"Maybe, but I set a new record."

"Records aren't going to keep you healthy."

"Neither will you throwing a wild pitch at my head."

My cheeks flushed. My insides trembling, reverberating down through my twitching hands. Bryce burst out laughing like a fool. He gave me a good, hard smack in the back. "You should've seen your face, Coop! It was priceless."

"I'm just surprised you would joke about something like that," I replied.

"Hey man, you can't take life too seriously."

"Whatever."

"It's true. I think will help those ladies with their long toss. You're more than welcome to join me. Oh, I forgot. You're a married man."

I snickered at Bryce while I punched the palm of my mitt.

"Lighten up, will ya?"

"Tired, I guess."

Bryce gave me a sly wink and jogged over to the lovely ladies in the outfield. I went back to the dorm. Alison called to tell me she wasn't feeling well as was staying in for the night. I took a long, hot shower, washing away the sweat and dirt of the field. I wiped away the steam from the mirrors and stared at myself. Analyzed every inch of my face.

It was as though I wasn't even looking at myself, but a stranger who had become more foreign with each passing day.

I noticed the new lines on my face and the bags under my eyes accompanied by my pale complexion. I was twenty-two, but felt older, but not the least bit wiser. Confused, if anything.

I brushed my teeth and changed into sweatpants and a shirt.

"Yo!" A voice boomed from the shower stalls. I turned to find Zach, wearing only boxers. Everything was proudly on display, from his well-rounded biceps to his lean abs. I looked back at the mirror, clutching my towel closer and vowing to spend an extra hour in the gym tomorrow. He took a piss in one of the urinals and washed his hands in the sink next to mine before giving me a salute.

"Oh captain my captain," Zach said while grabbing a towel and snapping it on my backside.

"You heard already?" I said trying to take the towel away.

"Word goes around pretty quick," Zach replied.

"I suppose it does."

"You don't seem too excited about it," Zach said.

"It was unexpected. How do you feel about it?"

Zach shrugged.

"Or do you care?"

"It doesn't matter what I think. I'm just the cog in the wheel of this fine institution we call Tampa State. I don't ask why things happen the way they do, I just accept it," Zach said.

"Not exactly a rousing endorsement."

"Coach should've run it by us first. I'm a firm believer in democracy. Without some moral code to follow, how the hell would we make sense of this world? Which is why we need to have a team meeting."

"Coach already made his decision," I said.

"How do you feel about it?" Zach asked.

"I don't know," I said, splashing my face with cold water.

"Just okay?"

"Look, what do you want?"

"There are important matters to discuss, Coop."

"And what might those be?"

"You know what I'm talking about."

"No, I don't."

"Do I have to spell it out for you, Coop?"

I threw my toothpaste and brush in my bag in disgust. "I don't I want to hear this." I turned to head back to my dorm before Zach grabbed me by the arm. I shoved him away. "Hey, Coop, wild pitch or not, you nearly killed Bryce last year with that fastball of yours. It shook a lot of the guys up. With coach making you captain the team needs to be confident you're up for it. We have too much at stake this season. We're seniors, Coop. For some of us it's our last shot at a winner."

"I told you everything. The pitch just got away from me."

"That's fine, but you must make your case in front of the rest of the team. It's only fair, considering the circumstances."

I wanted him to smoke me out already, to lift this burden off me, but I became a prisoner, held by my own self-preservation. Zach crossed his arms and leaned against the bathroom wall.

"I heard you that day at the hospital when you were with Bryce. What did you mean by that? Not being sure if you felt bad about it or not?"

I clenched the edge of the sink. "You spied on me?"

"No. I happened to drop in on your conversation. And you didn't answer my question."

"I was confused. If you recall I had a bad day." I left for my dorm. Zach followed.

"So did Bryce," he said.

"Why don't you just come out and say it? You think I did it on purpose, don't you?"

"I never said that. It's important that we clear things up in front of the guys. We owe it to Bryce and the team. It shook a lot of the guys up. It probably was one of reasons why we didn't even make the playoffs."

"Oh. So now it's my fault we didn't make the playoffs."

"I'm not saying that. But when you see one of your own lying in a pool of his own blood with his face caved in, that's going to fuck you up a. None of us have ever seen anything like that before. It's scary when you begin to question your own mortality; Coop. Being captain is a big responsibility. You're a leader on this team now. You know this is the right thing to do."

I glared at Zach and shut the door behind me, sequestering myself in my tiny room. I could see Zach's shadow prowling underneath the door. I crawled in bed and pulled the thin blankets around me. Through the sheets I could hear the telltale creak of the door swinging open. I rolled my eyes.

"What?!" I yelled. Zach's lips were pursed, his eyes fixed at me. He stood there, shirtless, with his arms crossed and veins bulging out of his forearms. "Look. I'm sorry OK. You gotta understand, behind this bohemian exterior, I do believe there are certain principles that need to be followed. Without some rules the whole world would go to hell if it hasn't already. Do you understand?"

I nodded and looked at my watch. "Let me feel your pulse?" Zach asked, pinching my wrist. "Dude, you're going a mile a minute. You're really tense."

"I'm a little stressed with school. That's all."

Zach snapped his fingers. "I got just the trick."

I followed him to his dorm. Zach shut the door behind him and took out the yoga mat beneath his bed and laid it out on the floor. He popped in a CD into his stereo, blaring meditation music. I admit it got me to relax. "What is this?" I asked.

"Sit down on the floor," Zach ordered.

"No way."

"I'm serious. It'll just take a few minutes. It will help you relax. Trust me. "

I sat down on the yoga mat. He instructed me to close my eyes and relax. When I shut them, all I could sense was my breathing and Zach's presence in the room. "Focus on your breathing. Listen to the sound of my voice. Big deep breaths."

I inhaled and exhaled, my lungs heaving slowly with every breath. I felt Zach sit behind me. I turned my head. "What are you doing?" I asked.

"Hey, you're not the only one that meditates around here. I have to get my time in, too. Just relax."

I became more entranced with every deep breath I took. My body felt lighter. My mind calm. I admit it was soothing to just be. I stopped hearing Zach's voice. I continued focusing on my breathing as he instructed when the hairs in the back of my neck stand. My breathing became shallow again when his hand ran across my chest. It took me a moment to realize what he was doing, the subtle touch of his hand grazing my chest awoke me from my meditative state.

I jumped from the yoga, shoving Zach in the process, knocking him to the floor. I stood over him while I looked at his confused expression. "What's wrong?" He said picking himself off the floor. "Are you OK?"

"Look. I'm fine. I think... I should be going."

"Don't go. Please."

"I'm feeling tired. I'll see ya tomorrow. Alright?"

Zach nodded, his eyes wide with shock, pleading with me to say something else. I shut the door when Bryce leaped out from the corner of the hallway and scared the shit out of me. "Don't do that!" I yelled.

"Ha! I got you good didn't I. What were you and Zach doing? Jerking off?"

"Don't you have anything else better to do?"

OK, mister sensitive. Where are you going?"

"To get a soda, if that's OK with you?" I said marching down hallway to the soda machine at the end of the hall.

# Chapter 10

The season was fast approaching as we began regular season practice. It was five a.m. and I wanted to crawl underneath my bed sheets hoping the day would go away. It should be criminal for people to be up that early in the morning. The sun rose over the bay. It was a picturesque sight as Bryce and I made our way to the gymnasium, changed and entered the pool area for our pre-practice swim. The water was freezing. It woke me up better than the cup of coffee Bryce and I grabbed earlier that morning.

The team took turns, swimming in between the roped lanes of the pool. Most of us weren't great swimmers, but of course Bryce was the exception. He flowed through the water effortlessly, like everything else in his life. Effortless. When my turn came, I dove into the pool, stretched my arms and kicked my legs, propelling myself through the water as hard as I could. Bryce waited for me at the end of the pool, his hand outstretched to help, mocking my inferiority. I refused his hand as I pulled myself up out of that damn cold water, More than refused, actually, I slapped it away. Bryce was taken aback for a moment, surprised, stealing away that stupid grin. My blood boiled with rage. "What, too slow today?" I shoved him. He nearly slipped on the wet floor before he shoved me back.

I skidded on the tiles, landing on my back. I lept onto my feet. I wanted to hit him. It just felt right to. Coach Dawson and a few others players held us back before I could even clench a fist.

"Both of you, come with me!" Coach was irate. We followed him outside to the darkly lit hallway next to the locker room. "What the hell was that all about?"

Neither of us said anything. We stared at each other. Bryce's astonished expression was priceless.

"I think it was just a misunderstanding, Coach," I said.

"Misunderstanding?"

"I took a joke the wrong way. That's all," I said.

"Is that what happened?"

Bryce, still confused, took his time to respond. "I guess."

"You guess?" Coach Dawson probed.

"What Coop said."

"Let's get one thing straight. You two are seniors and leaders on this team, so start acting like it. This is an important season for us, and if I find that you two are becoming a problem, I will make sure your asses are sitting on the bench the rest of the season. I don't want to have this conversation again."

Coach Dawson returned to the pool. Bryce was still astonished. "What's wrong with you?"

"Nothing."

"Nothing?"

"I'm sorry. Okay?"

"Whatever," Bryce sniffed.

We made our way back to the pool. Bryce dove in first. I pretended not to see him, but I knew Zach was watching me from across the pool as I waited for my turn to swim.

Bryce ignored me for the rest of practice, both in the pool and on the field. There was an awkwardness between us that wasn't there before. Bryce practiced his throws to second as players took turns bunting.

Two shadows sat in the stands, watching our every move. Both Patrick Buckhorn and Janet Marquis, the University President, were swathed in dark windbreakers, huddled against the early morning chill. It was rare to ever see Janet at a game, let alone a practice. They both wore dark sunglasses, so it was hard to make out if they were enjoying themselves. I doubt they were, at least Janet, for that matter.

The field grew warmer as practice went on. Janet and Patrick went to the fence near the backstop. Coach Dawson jogged from the first base line to meet them there. I stayed in the outfield, shagging fly balls, taking a break from throwing bullpen. The sun bore down on me as the morning turned to afternoon, making it hard to see the flys coming my way.

Zach jogged over as I caught a sharp line drive that curved in its trajectory. I sprinted to my left and caught the liner. The ball popping the web of my glove.

"Nice catch," Zach said.

"Thanks."

Zach took a few flys himself and rifled some balls back to the infield. "You and Bryce okay?"

"Sure."

"Didn't seem that way back at the pool."

"It was a misunderstanding."

"Does he know that?"

"I suppose."

"Right." Zach's droopy eyes stared into my face. "Listen. About that night."

"Forget it," I said hurling a ball to the infield.

"Did you tell anyone?" He said.

A line drive rocketed from home plate. I shuffled my feet to the right and snagged it, the ball smacking my glove nice and hard, throwing it back to the cut off man.

"Did you?" Zach repeated. "No. I didn't. Besides, what's the big deal?"

Zach leaned in and whispered. "It's not out there. Here with these jocks, I don't think it would go over very well."

I nodded and sighed. "You're secret is safe with me."

Zach smiled and smacked me on the back. "I appreciate it. You coming out with us tonight? We're going go-carting at Malibu Grand Prix."

"I'm going out with Alison tonight."

"Bring her along."

"I don't think she would like go-carts."

"What would make you say that?"

"She's has unique tastes."

"A true bohemian," Zach replied.

"I guess you can call her that."

It seemed every time Zach spoke to me he had an ulterior motive. He acted as if our conversation in the bathroom never took place. He covered it up with yet another secret I had to endure. A lifetime history of questions ran through my mind as I tried to hold together my sanity, concluding that not everyone is who they seem to be.

Coach Dawson left Patrick and Janet at the fence and blew his whistle. The team lined up at left field. We sprinted from one end of the outfield to the other. My body ached from our morning swim, but the pain felt good. Bryce was at the opposite end, beating out the rest of us. I sprinted harder, trying to catch up, but he beat me every time. Just like when we jogged together in the mornings. He was always one step ahead.

After Coach Dawson ended practice, I made my way to the athletic building when a hand reached out from behind me. Patrick's pearly white teeth broke through his wide grin. "Coop. Got a moment?"

"Sure," I said.

"I'm sure you know who this is, Janet Marquis."

She stuck out her hand. I took my time, taking off my glove and the batting glove on my catching hand. Janet coughed with impatience.

Her hand was limp when I shook it, and she immediately wiped her hand on her blouse afterwards. "Looked good out there in practice. I saw you throw bullpen earlier," Patrick said.

"Arm feels about right. Should be ready for the season."

Patrick put his arm on my shoulder. "Janet, Cooper here is going to help lead this team to a NCAA championship this year," Patrick said.

"I would hope so," Janet responded.

"Are you a baseball fan, Janet?" I said.

"I find it intriguing, and you can call me Ms. Marquis," she said, perturbed.

Patrick did most of the talking from then on. Janet rolled her eyes from all the jock talk. Patrick at least understood what it was to be out on the field and compete.

Janet stepped aside to take a phone call, and Patrick turned to me. He was a large man, much bigger than I. An intimidating presence, sculpted from his days of playing football. "Coop, you think you're at your best?"

"My best?"

"Yes. Do you think you're playing to the best of your ability? Is there room for improvement?"

"I suppose you can always get better."

Patrick smiled showing off his white teeth.

"You're an important part of this team, Coop. But I need you to push a little harder. That goes for all of you. I need you at your best. Can you do that?"

"I thought I was already at my best?"

Buckhorn shrugged. "You can do better."

Push. Ninety mph. Play harder. The lingo of athletic motivation swirled in my mind. The magic number I hit only once, and that was when I beamed Bryce in the face.

After practice I took a shower and went to the library to study. The thrill of Accounting. It was boring, but at least the language made sense. Once I finished studying I relaxed in the student commons at Orsini Hall. I flipped through the channels on the large flat-screen TV. The war was waging in Iraq. College didn't seem real in comparison. An alternate reality where adulthood was staved off for the sake of higher education when your real education would start after it was over. I wasn't sure how I would make it in the real world. I had plans, but it was easy to make plans in college. Outside the walls of Tampa State, plans could break down. The ever-elusive black swan that no one sees coming. I knew where I stood in college. There was structure, order, a routine. Out there, anything goes. It was a terrifying thought.

I took a nap on the couch. No one was around. The windows allowed the sun to shine through, casting a warm glow on the couch I lay on. I wanted to sleep for only fifteen minutes, but when I woke up and checked my watch, I saw that it was five. I still felt groggy. I could've slept a few more hours. I must have been exhausted.

I was supposed to meet Alison at her dorm at six. I went up to my dorm to change. Bryce was sitting at his desk, doing homework for once. Patrick must've said something about his grades. He ignored me when I came in, glued to his studies. "Pigs really can fly now," I said.

He kept his eyes on his Principles of Finance book.

"Do you need help?" I asked.

"Maybe," he said. "I'll let you know."

"You still mad at me?"

He sighed and turned toward me. "About what?"

"Come on, you know what."

"Forget it. No biggie," Bryce said. "Where are you off to?"

"Going out with Alison."

"Oh," Bryce said, rolling his eyes.

"You going go-carting tonight with the guys?" I asked.

"Nah, probably stay in. Maybe catch up on homework."

"Okay, where's Bryce and what did you do with him?"

"This is my last year. I want to end my academic career with a bang."

"Baseball comes second this time?"

"I think both are in the running, Coop. How long you going to be out with Alison for?"

"We're going to an art festival later. She has to wake up early for class tomorrow so I won't be out too late."

"Let's go drinking later."

"I thought you said you want to end your academic career with a bang?"

"Who said you can't drink and get good grades?"

"Good point."

I told Bryce that I would call him when I was done with my date with Alison. We ate dinner at The Pelican. It was close by and I figured we should splurge. The food wasn't too bad, either. After dinner we took a stroll to the botanical gardens. The evening was cool, a pleasant relief from the scorching day. When we arrived, we found a sprawl of tents glowing from the soft twinkling lights, illuminating the colorful swaths of art. It was a wild sprawl with some tents cutting through the flora of the garden. I worried the miniature city would trample the delicate ambiance the garden created.

Alison took her time analyzing the artwork, asking my opinion of each piece. I nodded my head, pretending Alison's opinion of each piece made the slightest bit of sense. The garden was a cornucopia of flowers, tropical plants and foliage, decorating the area with a lushness variety of distinct color and plants that made it far more interesting to admire than the artwork on display at the festival.

"You don't like this, do you?" Alison asked.

"I do."

"Liar," she replied.

"What makes you think I'm lying?"

"Your ears are turning red."

"Is that right?"

"Mmm-hmm."

"Don't mmm-hmm me," I said.

"Do you even know what you're looking at half the time?" she asked.

"The paintings?"

"Yes."

I pointed at a painting of a lighthouse overlooking what looked like Chesapeake Bay. A small fishing boat with a fisherman inside sat still in the water beneath the lighthouse by the shore. The fisherman had his line cast, wearing a raincoat. "You see. That's a lighthouse overlooking the bay with a fishing boat by the shore."

"And the fisherman?" Alison asked.

"What about him?"

"You only see what's obvious. There is always more to a painting than what meets the eye," Alison said.

"So then what do you see?"

She pressed her hand against her chin, taking a moment to interpret the painting. Alison looked beautiful. She was real, but had layers of complexity making her all the more tantalizing. I reminded myself of her secret, of her walking up the stairs with that boy, but it only seemed to intensify my desire for her.

"He's dying," Alison said, interrupting my reverie

"Who?"

"The fisherman." She gestured towards the tiny man in the tiny boat.

"And how can you tell he's dying?"

"He's alone. Loneliness is like death."

"That's sort of morbid, isn't it?"

"Like I said, it's how I interpret it. That's the beauty of art. Each person has their own perspective."

We moved on to the next tent. As we entered we were greeted by a longhaired hipster with thick black-rimmed glasses. "Hey guys. Make yourselves at home. Let me know if there's anything you like," he said.

There were only a few paintings, but one jumped out at me from across the tent. The black background contrasted with a strikingly white face, which seemed to be melting. Its features were exaggerated, its eyes bloodshot, black and large like oversized grapes. The nose was small and limp. But behind the morbid features was a grim smile as if there was some sort of joy behind it. I stared at the painting for a while as Alison spoke with the hipster. I was mesmerized by the painting. It pulled me in. I stared at it if I was looking in a mirror. The painting was all that mattered. I entered a trance, looking inward, staring at myself.

I felt a smack on the back of my head. "Hey, you awake?" Alison said. "I called your name three times."

"Sorry. Just looking at the painting."

"You like the painting, huh?" the hipster said standing behind us. "I call it 'Metamorphosis'."

"Really, why is that?" Alison said.

"We all go through some sort of transformation based on what we feed our subconscious from the conscious mind. We go through a transformation fueled by our own subconscious without us even realizing it, even if it's into something we don't want to be or fully comprehend."

"So you're saying you can become somebody else without even being aware of it?"

"Exactly! How many times have you heard stories of good people who do bad things? Sometimes there's just something ingrained inside all of us that entices us to do good or bad deeds. Our brains are split into the conscious and subconscious minds. Our conscious mind feeds images, words and other thoughts into the subconscious mind. We feed it positive material, our overall being changes for the better. But when we feed it negative thoughts, our beings go bad. Like our souls rot from the inside. But it's how our thoughts manifest themselves that is the big mystery. Why people do what they do. You can become a bad person without even being aware of it or having any control over your transformation. Maybe external factors have something to do with it, but we all have a dark side, whether we like it or not."

"Wow, trippy," Alison said.

"I know! Sell it to you for one hundred and fifty bucks," the hipster, said rubbing his hands together. Alison twitched her lips, contemplating the purchase. "We'll think about it," she said.

"How about your boyfriend?" he asked.

"I'm not her boyfriend," I said bluntly.

The hipster, embarrassed, offered a discounted price of one hundred and twenty dollars.

"No thanks," I replied.

"Let me know if you change your mind."

We left the tent. Alison looked at me like I was one of those paintings,. I noticed her look. "No labels. Remember?"

I dropped off Alison back at her dorm just as it began to rain. I sprinted across the campus, hitting puddles of water that drenched my shoes and the hems of my jeans.

Bryce was in our dorm, just back from the gym. "Couldn't beat the rain, huh?" he said.

"It's pouring. Don't think it's a great night to go out," I said.

Bryce pulled a cooler out from underneath his bed. "Always have a contingency plan."

We went to the student lounge. The last time I got drunk was at a frat party freshman year and the only thing I remember was waking up naked in Clearwater beach with a towel wrapped around my head surrounded by empty beer bottles. The beer was disgusting and warm, but at least it was cheap. We played pool. Best out of three. We won one a piece. I scratched, losing the last match.

"Good game," Bryce said, chugging down another beer. I followed suit, working my way from buzzed to borderline-drunk. We sat on one of the couches of the student lounge, the very same couch I'd taken a nap in earlier that day. I could've fallen asleep again, but Bryce kept me up, talking up his night with a junior Biology major who'd crafted an itinerary just for their date. They went to dinner. The European Café, a semi-expensive restaurant that recently opened near campus, followed by a romantic comedy that Bryce thought was horrid, and then drinks in downtown Tampa at a wine bar. Bryce wasn't exactly an epicurean when it came to wine, or anything else for that matter." His speech became slurred. "It was brutal, Coop. Brutal. I mean, shit, she didn't let me kiss her goodnight. And I paid for everything! I'm not made of money."

"None of us are," I said with lifted eyebrows.

The barrage of raindrops beat furiously against the window as a storm raged outside. The sky lit up blue and white as thunder crashed in the distance. "Hell of a storm," Bryce said. I stood to look outside and watched the rain hit the window.

"Bryce."

"Yeah."

"I gotta tell you something," I said.

"Shoot," Bryce said, yawning and then taking a sip of beer.

I slowly crushed the empty beer can in my hand, the aluminum cracking beneath my fingers as the can crumpled in the palm of my hand. "It's about what happened last season, when I hit you."

"Oh, not again," Bryce said stumbling as he went to get another beer from the 12-pack he left sitting on top of the pool table. "Look, Coop, we already talked about it. No hard feelings, okay? It was just an accident."

Rain trickled down on the window pane. The raindrops sagged and ran, like that 'Metamorphosis' painting at the fair..

"What if it wasn't an accident?" I said.

Bryce seemed sober for a moment, holding the can of beer in his hand.

"That day. When I hit you. I remember not feeling much of anything. Not shock, remorse, pain. Nothing. It was like I wasn't even there. I don't know why, but that's how I felt ever since."

"What on Earth are you talking about, Coop? You're not making sense."

"It wasn't an accident, Bryce." I turned to face him, the storm raging behind me. "I did it on purpose."

There was a moment of absolute silence. Seconds seemed like minutes.

"Ha!" Bryce yelled, laughing as he popped open his beer. "You're too much, Coop. That's a good one."

"You're not listening to me."

Bryce grimaced as sipped from his can. "I hate warm beer." He picked up what was left of the 12-pack, realized the two remaining beers were too warm for his taste. "Wanna go for a beer run?" He said stumbling around the room.

"Aren't you listening to one word I'm saying?"

"Coop, you're drunk. I'm drunk. Neither one of us are making a lot of sense."

"Bryce, I'm telling you that what happened that day wasn't an accident." Reality was setting in and becoming crystal clear. Bryce was oblivious because he was too drunk.

"Coop, you need to stop, okay? Get over it."

"Haven't you ever been the least bit curious?"

Bryce belched before heading to the door. "No. You're my friend, and you're drunk." He staggered out into the hall, knocking over the fire extinguisher that hung on the wall.

The rain continued beating on the windowpane behind me. I looked outside again, at the water overflowing from the fountain.

There was a figure standing beside it. I recognized the black and yellow jogging suit. *Is it him?* I asked myself.

The figure and I stared at each other for a good minute before I ran outside. It rained so hard it hurt. The figure was gone. I looked frantically. I saw something hiding behind a cluster of bushes several feet away. As I approached, the shadowy figure jumped out and ran. I sprinted after him, but Miguel had darted off into the night, as mysteriously as he first appeared in front of Orsini Hall.

# Chapter 11

We started the season with eight wins in a row against Bentley, Georgia College and Southern Indiana. Despite starting the season with eight wins in a row, Coach Dawson continued to push us. One too many errors, not enough runs. The man was hard to please, but we were winning, and that's what mattered.

Buckhorn visited the clubhouse frequently to check up on us. He was practically a coach himself, going out on the field and giving us pointers, even though he had never touched a baseball in his life.

Bryce seemed to be fond of him. They were cut from the same cloth. Two superior athletes who understood what it was like to be great.

Bryce was having a stellar season. By early March we were sixteen and one. He was batting .348 with ten home runs and forty RBIs. He was on a tear. The injury inflicted on him was irrelevant to his performance, and the scouts noticed. Buckhorn arranged a meeting with a scout from the Pirates.

I started the season with a four and one record, and still hadn't reached ninety again.

Zach clocked me whenever he sneaked the radar gun into the

dugout. My arm felt good. Bryce and I communicated well. He understood me, at least as far as my pitching was concerned. I liked the hard stuff. Blowing a guy away with a fastball was satisfying; watching him grimace at knowing his best wasn't enough.

I didn't see Bryce much off the field. He began dating a Marketing major named Dawn he met in between classes at the College of Business, and he spent much of his time with Buckhorn. These two were like best pals, laughing and shooting the breeze before and after every game. It left a bad taste in my mouth. I was as confused as I had ever been. *Why did Bryce have to come back?*

It would have made things so much easier if he'd stayed away. I was a mess of emotions. There were days I would get physically sick. I would lie in bed, not wanting to move hoping no one bother me. Thursday afternoon I turned up the air conditioning in the room. I lay underneath the sheets, appreciating the dark, cool air.

I slept in an amber glow from the rays of the setting sun. The tranquil moment was interrupted when Bryce burst into the room. The door nearly flew off its hinges. He was filled with excitement, like a child who just received a new toy. "Big news, buddy! Really big news."

"Could you least knock?" I grumbled.

He tossed a manila envelope onto my lap. I rubbed my eyes and put on my reading glasses that I keep on the nightstand beside my bed. "Open it," Bryce said.

I pulled out what looked like a contract. There were signatures adorning the first few pages. I noticed the Pittsburgh Pirates letterhead on the top of the page. "The Pirates?"

"I got signed today."

"You got signed?"

"Crazy, isn't it?"

"Yes, it is," I said.

"Buckhorn did most of the negotiating."

"Can he do that?" I asked.

"How the fuck am I supposed to know? But I got signed, pal. I'm going to the pros!"

"Congratulations," I said, plopping my head back on the pillow.

"Hey, what's wrong with you?"

"Me? Nothing."

"Hey, cheer up, Coop. Look, you're having a hell of a season. It won't be long before I'm hitting bombs off of you in the bigs," Bryce laughed.

"Sure," I said.

"We need to celebrate."

To celebrate anything worthwhile, it was best to do it in Ybor City. That night we all went to an Irish bar called O'Malleys, a hole in the wall with an aged wooden interior that looked like a bygone speakeasy. Bryce held court near the center of the bar with Dawn hanging off his arm. Alison watched the spectacle with an amused smirk, and I nursed my beer.

At first I didn't speak much. I just watched Allison's smile and laughter while she played with the bangs of her hair. We locked eyes with each other and smiled. Her secret kept popping into my mind, but at least for that moment, being with her was all that mattered. It was at that point I knew I was in love with her.

I felt myself come alive whenever I was in the same room as her. Every time I saw her it was like the first time. My throat would constrict just trying to muster up enough words to say something. Even with all the secrets, she made my world just a little bit better, relieving the growing pain gnawing at my soul. I loved her damn it, and I hated myself for it.

"You alright?" Alison asked. "You're sweating."

I wiped my brow with the napkin I took from the table.

"Hot in here," I said gripping her hand underneath the table as Dawn and Alison gossiped, running my fingers along her knuckles over and over again. Zach, Bryce, Samson, and I drank our cheap beers and discussed what would be our glory days when it was all said and done.

"To Bryce and the Pirates. God help them," Zach said as we raised a toast with our frothy mugs. The glass mugs chimed in unison, with some of the foamy beer spilling over onto the wooden table.

"Just to warn you, Dawn. Bryce here doesn't like foreplay," Samson joked to Dawn.

"I noticed. He's not very good at it even when he tries," Dawn said.

"Hey hey, easy there," Bryce objected.

Dawn sat on his lap and kissed him and took a sip of his beer. I turned to Alison and put my arm around her shoulder. She gave me a wet kiss and ran her fingers through my hair.

"Say, Coop, when are *you* getting signed?" Samson asked with his Cheshire Cat grin. I had the urge to throw my glass mug full of beer at his face.

"Coop's got a couple of scouts looking at him as we speak," Bryce said.

"I see all of you are having a good time."

The voice took me aback. I wasn't expecting to see him here. It was a total surprise. The group of us turned to the direction of the voice that had boomed behind us. He smiled, showing off his pearly white teeth. Patrick Buckhorn dressed in brand new jeans and a pressed button down shirt. His hair slicked back, wearing the subtle tan of a few hours at the beach, or a quick stop at a tanning salon. His flashy Rolex glimmered underneath the hot bar lights. Bryce got up and gave him one of those big bear hugs that seemed to last an eternity, making it somewhat awkward to the rest of us who were wondering why the Athletic Director was having a drink with us students.

Patrick Buckhorn pulled up a chair and sat beside Bryce. The server came by and took his drink order, bringing him back rum and coke. We were sudden introverts, minding our own business while we watched Buckhorn enjoy his drink.

"Nice place. Reminds me of bar I went to back at Notre Dame. A hole in the wall just like this."

"Patrick here played football for the Irish," Bryce said.

*Now they're on a first name basis?*

"Irish, huh?" Samson said. "I'm a USC fan."

"Sorry to hear that," Patrick responded.

"How about another toast? To Tampa State baseball and to a NCAA championship," Bryce said.

"I'll drink to that," replied Patrick. We toasted again, the chime of our glasses as sharp and distinct as before.

"Speaking of NCAA, isn't it against the rules for school officials to be fraternizing with students?" I said.

To be honest, I didn't know squat about NCAA rules, but I figured there had to be something about relations between school officials and students, especially when alcohol was involved. Patrick took a sip of his drink and puckered his lips, setting the glass down on the wet paper napkin. "The young man knows the rules, but the old man knows the exceptions." Patrick winked.

"Oliver Wendell Holmes!" Alison said excitingly. I turned to Alison with a puzzled expression. "Oh. He was a Chief Justice under the Roosevelt administration. Learned about him in an American History class."

"Very good. Alison, right?" Patrick asked.

"Yes," she cooed.

Patrick seemed to rule the room with his charm. He talked about his days playing at Notre Dame and the NFL. He patrolled the room armed with his ability to talk a good game. It was the investment banker in him, knowing how to survey his surroundings and look at the multiple angles of every person or situation. He was good. Bryce couldn't stop talking about getting signed by the Pirates, but Dawn didn't care too much for it.

The rest of the table drifted away. Zach and Samson went to play darts, Patrick stepped outside to take a phone call. Bryce came over to Alison and me. We were drinking at the bar, watching a soccer game on the big flat screen that hung above the bar. The bartender, a short blonde with tattoos of dragons on her arms, mixed various drinks with what can best be described as organized chaos, serving the cocktails with dizzying efficiency. I watched her performance while Bryce and Alison talked amongst themselves. "When do you report?" I asked Bryce.

"After the season. I'll be in double AA mid-July. They want me working on my throwing mechanics first. Work out some kinks in my swing. If I play well enough, I might be in the pros by next season."

"That's ambitious," I said.

"Yeah, well, it's all about confidence, Coop."

"And you're just brimming with it."

"Hey, you gotta be confident, playing this game. Of all people, you should know that."

"I guess I'm more modest. This game can humble you pretty quick, Bryce," I said.

Bryce's eyes squinted at my remark, drinking his beer and opting to watch the game.

"Did I miss anything?" Patrick asked, returning from his phone call.

"Not really," I said.

"So, Coop, I've been looking at your stats. Impressive."

"Thanks."

"What do you think about your ERA?" Patrick asked.

"3.04, last time I checked."

"Yes, and?"

"And what?"

"What do you think of it?"

"I'll tell you what I think. It can be better. A hell of a lot better."

"It's good, but not good enough for an NCAA championship, Coop. You're our best pitcher. I've read your scouting report, you are in the top ten in strikeouts. But I think we can work on your speed."

A glowing red ninety flashed my mind. My heart raced as if I were on the mound. "Speed?"

"You're a finesse pitcher. That's good. But we can do better. I want you blowing people away. More strikeouts, more wins. Championship. Get me?"

"You make it sound so easy."

"Bryce and I will work with you."

"You and Bryce?"

"I've been working with him already. He's got great stuff," Bryce replied, turning his attention away from the TV.

"We can make him better. You hitting the weight room?" asked Patrick.

"When I can. I jog a lot."

"Stop jogging. We need you to hit the weight room. More strength and conditioning. I'll work with you."

"I sort of have a routine," I replied.

Alison giggled "You boys and your sports."

"I take it you don't like sports?" Buckhorn asked.

"Especially baseball," Alison replied. "But this guy makes it tolerable." Alison nudged me in the arm with her elbow.

"How long have you two been dating?"

"Almost a year," I replied.

Alison excused herself and went to the bathroom.

"You like Alison?" asked Patrick.

"I do. She's different from all the other girls I've dated."

"How so?"

"She keeps me on my toes. Sometimes I don't know if it's a good or bad thing, but it works I suppose."

Patrick motioned Bryce and me to lean in closer to him as if we were in a huddle waiting for him to call out a play. "Word of advice. Women and athletics don't mix. I'm talking from personal experience here," Patrick said.

"Really?" Bryce said, looking around to see if Dawn noticed. "I mean, I like Dawn and all. Hell, she's put up with me for a whole month. That's a keeper in my book."

Patrick's demeanor shifted. He wasn't the charming "one-of-the-guys" who'd strolled into the bar an hour ago He became controlling and decisive in his words.

He stressed that it was a bad idea for us to be involved with the opposite sex. He was very specific about it. Single himself, he hated baggage, as he called it. He kept talking for what seemed like an eternity while I waited for Alison to return.

But what I learned about Patrick was he was a man of few distractions, and he wanted to keep it that way, both his personal life and in Tampa State's Athletic program.

Alison returned. His demeanor changed to the charmer again. He got off his stool and offered it to Alison. She politely accepted and sat on the stool between Patrick and Bryce. I excused myself to the bathroom, and Bryce followed me.

"I like Dawn," Bryce said.

"Then stay with her."

"But Patrick said—"

"Who cares what Patrick said?"

"I mean, maybe he has a point. He got me the Pirates deal after all."

"That doesn't mean he owns you. For God's sake, don't you have the slightest bit of common sense? You're oblivious," I said sharply.

Bryce retreated to the men's stall. I finished and began washing my hands. I heard flatulence boom from the stall, followed by childish laughter. "Classy," I said rolling my eyes.

I bobbed and weaved my way through the throng of people at the bar. Zach and Samson were still throwing darts. I found Patrick and Alison in deep conversation. Alison listened intensively, leaning towards him and laughed at almost everything he said. He was a charmer. I felt my chest tighten, watching the two of them in deep conversation. Like with the painting, I was in a trance, this time from rage. A drunk middle-aged man bumped into me, spilling some of his beer on my shirt. I snapped back into reality.

"Sorry, we need to go."

I grabbed Alison by the arm.

"But...."

"I have to wake up early."

"Game against Georgia, right?"

"Yeah."

"Good idea. Get some rest," Buckhorn said.

Alison and I exited the bar before Patrick shouted my name. "Coop." I turned to him. "Remember what we talked about."

I didn't nod. I didn't speak a word. I looked into his bright smile and then left the bar, feeling disgusted.

"We could've stayed a little longer," Alison said. "It's still early."

"Sorry. Long day. What were you two talking about?"

"He's quite the literary buff. I was surprised, coming from a jock."

"Everybody is full of surprises."

We went back to her dorm. Alison shoved me on the bed. She bit her lip in delight, throwing herself on top of me, kissing me with fervor. As Alison took her bra, the door swung open with Joanna dropping the stack of books she was carrying. Alison covered herself as she lay topless on her bed. "Ever heard of a hotel?" her roommate exclaimed.

"Joanna. I thought you weren't coming till later."

"The study session ended early. Do I have to knock every time I come in? Seriously this is getting to be annoying." Joanna said picking up her books off the floor.

"You don't have to get all worked up over it."

"I have a group study session at seven tomorrow morning!" She said slamming the books on her desk.

"Another one?" Alison asked.

"You're obviously not Pre-Law."

"Maybe I should go," I said.

"No, stay. Joanna, you need to get a grip."

"I want him to go," Joanna insisted.

I got off the bed and buttoned my jeans. Joanna stood by the door with her arms crossed and bags underneath her eyes. I could tell she despised me. I empathized with that. I saw a little bit of myself in her as I walked passed her and turned the doorknob.

"This isn't a co-ed dorm. I should report you," she said.

I turned and gave her a cold stare while watching Alison out of the corner of my eye, sitting on the bed, waiting to see what I would do next. I think Alison liked the anticipation. Joanna stepped back, intimidated.

"Shouldn't you be in bed?" I said.

Joanna cocked her head with wide eyes.

"I'll call you tomorrow," I told Alison before I left. I heard the two argue back and forth as I made my way down the hallway. I left wreckage in my wake, and I liked it.

# Chapter 12

We were on a three-game skid, losing to West Alabama. The Florida sun was brutal and intense. The field felt like scorched earth, crunching underneath my cleats. I pitched four scoreless innings before Tyler Johnson, the West Alabama cleanup hitter and right fielder, hit a towering home run I think is still orbiting the Earth's atmosphere. Our bats were silent throughout most of the game, mustering only two hits. Both by Bryce, who has been suffering from heat cramps. After the game he barely made it back to the dugout on his own.

Bryce peeled off his catcher's equipment, plopped himself behind the dugout and put a cold towel over his head. He didn't want anybody to see he was weak.

The heat had been unforgiving, but so was Coach Dawson. He berated us after the game. I'd never seen him that angry before. As the few fans in attendance left the stands, Patrick Buckhorn emerged into view, sitting on the edge of the last bleacher looking directly at our dugout, his eyes were hidden behind his expensive Ray Ban sunglasses. Coach made us run wind sprints in the outfield, except for Bryce, who was being looked at by the one of trainers.

"Why doesn't Bryce have to do wind sprints?" Samson cried.

"You can make up by doing his, since you're so concerned," Coach Dawson said.

After ten sprints, Coach Dawson blew his whistle and told us to hit the showers. Buckhorn walked towards us from the opposing dugout. He stood behind Coach Dawson, surprising him by patting him on the shoulder. His scowl was obvious to everyone. He took Coach Dawson aside. Patrick spoke with him briefly before Coach blew his whistle again.

"Alright. Ten more sprints," he said.

"Ten more!" Zach exclaimed.

Coach yelled for Bryce. "Sprints!" Bryce looked at the trainer. Bryce slowly got up and jogged over to us.

Buckhorn's scowl transformed to a grin as he watched us do wind sprints until we suffered from sheer exhaustion. A few of us puked in the outfield. Bryce finished, still beating out most of us.

"Alright, that's enough," said Coach.

Later Bryce was up and about in the dugout, drinking water with a moist towel around his head. He was a little light headed. "That was one too many sprints," he said.

"One too many," I agreed, nearly collapsing on the dugout. I reached for my bag and grabbed my water bottle, then took a large gulp. I heard a commotion near the dugout. Doug Lynn, the team trainer, was furious, yelling at both Buckhorn and Dawson.

"What are you trying to do, kill these kids? You know how hot it is out here! Bryce is dehydrated!"

"Calm down, Doug," Coach said.

"How can you tell me to calm down!? That was downright abuse. These kids haven't eaten anything in hours, and you pull that stunt!"

Buckhorn stood and listened, not saying a word. Motionless. Doug kicked a helmet that was on the floor, sending it over the dugout fence and onto the field.

"I want to speak to both of you," Patrick said to Bryce and me.

We followed him to the entrance of the clubhouse. I wondered which version of Patrick Buckhorn we were going to see. He crossed his arms, his massive forearms sticking out from the sleeves of his Tampa State polo shirt. "What happened out there?"

"We lost, obviously."

"Are you trying to be smart with me?" he snapped.

"It's just a rough patch. We'll get out of it," Bryce said.

"Have you looked at the standings? We're only one game ahead in first place. Georgia's nipping at our heels. Going on a three-game skid is unacceptable. You're better than that."

"We are," Bryce agreed.

"You still dating those girls?"

"What does that have to do with it?" I asked.

Patrick scoffed, "Women and sports don't mix."

"What we do off the field is none of your business," I said.

Patrick said nothing. He paced around for a moment. Without warning, he slammed his fist against the metal door of the clubhouse, leaving a small dent. His right hand was bruised, with blood coming out from cuts on his knuckles. He clenched his fist to make sure it wasn't broken.

He laughed and became the charmer again. "I hope you guys understand where I'm coming from on this. I'll be expecting you two in the weight room tomorrow. We got work to do."

Bryce and I agreed by just nodding our heads.

Bryce went back to the trainer to get extra ice packs. His body was beat up from the heat and a long series. He got some extra packs for me. My arm felt like Jell-o. I wasn't sure how either one of us would make it to the weight room tomorrow.

Later we talked to Coach Dawson about doing extra strength and conditioning training with Patrick. He seemed indifferent; saying that if he thought it would make us better, then do it. Doug was furious, but the last thing he wanted was a blemish on his record because he pissed off some hotshot Athletic Director, especially the likes of Patrick Buckhorn.

After practice we hit the showers and went to class. Future and Options and Financial Statement Analysis were the courses for the day and kept me plenty busy with homework. I studied with Alison in the library. Books that were as old as the school itself, with their musky smell, remained in their shelves like ghosts haunting those who studied in their presence. Alison kept tapping her pencil on the wood table like a drummer. It was very annoying.

"Would you stop that?" I said.

"Stop what?"

"That." I pointed to her pencil.

"Oh, sorry," she said.

She closed her literary textbook and just stared at me from across the table. I kept studying. Too much homework. Future and Options wasn't exactly a cakewalk.

"Hey," she said, smiling. "Wanna get out of here?"

"Now?"

"No, tomorrow. Yes, now. There's always time for homework."

I reminded her I had a Future and Options exam in a few days. But I thought a break would do me some good. We drove to this small beach off of the causeway that stretched between the interior of Tampa Bay and Clearwater. There was a small tiki bar and a jet ski rental stand that made us feel like we were on a Caribbean island, away from the hustle and bustle of civilization. The sun set over the gulf. The water tame with a few waves washing up against the shore. The sand felt coarse and smooth, still warm from the heat of the afternoon sun.

She sat in between my legs underneath a wool blanket we'd taken from my dorm. I kissed her forehead and wrapped my arms around her. "This is nice," she said.

"Yes, it is," I said.

We said little, just enjoying the sunset as day turned to night. There were a few beachgoers lying about or walking on the beach near the water, soaking their feet in wet sand as they walked past us. An old couple strolled past us. The wife staggered as she walked, but kept up with her husband who helped her along the beach.

"How long do you think they've been married?" I asked.

"How do you know they're married?" Alison asked.

"Wild guess, I suppose. But I forgot, you don't like labels."

"They could be cohabitating."

"Why don't we just imagine them celebrating their fiftieth wedding anniversary and they're as happy as they've ever been?" I said.

"You were always old fashioned."

"What's wrong with that?"

Alison paused for a moment and leaned the back of her head against my chest. "Nothing," she said.

Then she added, "We're graduating soon."

"Yes we are."

"I was thinking about going to grad school next fall."

"At Tampa State?" I asked.

"No, I was thinking New York. I would like to study film. NYU has a great masters program."

Oh," I said solemnly.

"What's the matter? I thought you would be happy."

"I suppose this whole thing is getting a bit complicated. Not that it wasn't already," I said.

She turned and wrapped her legs around me, and kissed me. "You could always visit me, you know."

"To New York?"

"Maybe Austin. Honestly, I have no idea where I'll end up. That's what makes it exciting."

"I don't know where I'll end up, either," I responded.

"That's what makes life interesting, don't you think?"

I sighed and stared out into the ocean.

"What's wrong?" Alison said.

"Nothing seems to bother you."

"What do you mean?"

She unwrapped her legs as I stood and wiped the sand off my jeans. "It seems like I'm just an afterthought to you. Like whatever it is we have is just based on convenience."

"You really believe that, Cooper?"

"All I know is that we've been together for over a year and you still look at our relationship as some way of stroking your own ego. Like you're afraid to commit to something."

She kicked sand at me, throwing me into a coughing fit "What the hell was that for!" I said with Alison inches from his face.

"Listen, Coop. I'm tired of having to explain myself to you. I don't know what more I can give you. I concede I may be difficult, but I have my reasons."

"What are reasons are those?"

"Hmm, try having a control freak as a father who tried to control every aspect of your life. From the college I wanted to go to to the boys I dated, I couldn't breath without his permission. My mom quit her career as a bank executive because my father thought it would be a distraction from her 'responsibilities' at home. I would watch her turn to pills just so she could make it through the day. Oh and don't let me forget my ex-boyfriend who I had to file a restraining order on because he thought it was cute to break into my apartment after I broke up with him and try to steal half my shit."

She took a deep breath, her shoulders shaking. "I'm not going to put my entire life on hold because of something I don't even know will work. I care about you, Cooper. I really do, and I don't want to lose what we have, but I'm not ready to give you what you want."

I sighed and ran my hand through her hair. "Alison, you're blaming me for things I had nothing to do with. I'm not your father or your ex-boyfriend."

Deep inside I wanted to tell Alison I loved her. I clenched her hand and held her in my arms. Her fingers grazed my face before she kissed me. "Let's just enjoy the moment and see where it goes. I'm tired of thinking about the future."

"Or the past," I said.

Frank Nunez

We rolled up our jeans and walked along the shore. The soapy water gurgled against the shore, submerging our feet in the frothy water of the Gulf of Mexico. An airliner's landing lights glimmered in the distance as it descended into Tampa International airport, a short distance from the beach. The engines of the 737 roared in our ears and deafened us to the sounds of the ocean waves.

# Chapter 13

At dawn Bryce, Pat Buckhorn, and I were in the weight room. The stench of iron hit my nostrils like a Mack Truck. The equipment was old and rusty, but it was adequate. Buckhorn hated the weight room. He wanted a state-of-the-art facility with the latest equipment, an indoor track, training rooms, and a hot and cold bath to treat sore muscles.

We spent most of our time doing bodyweight exercises, squats and other compound exercises. Buckhorn pushed us to our physical limits. My legs buckling while I tried to perform my last rep of a three hundred pound squat. I slammed the barbell on the squat rack. Bryce did a set, slamming the barbell on the rack then high-fiving Buckhorn like some cliché 80s montage.

"Ten to your five," Buckhorn said to me. I nodded my head and took a large gulp of water from my water bottle. My legs, not to mention knees, ached with pain. I could barely get myself back up to go to the locker room to change. Bryce reached out his hand and lifted me up from the rubber mat that made up the gym floor.

Coach Dawson saw us from the window that overlooked the hallway between the weight room and the gymnasium where the bouncing of basketballs from the pick-up game reverberated through the halls. He was carrying his usual blue coffee thermos.

I could tell that he was pissed off. Not because we were working out, but he was kept out of the loop. Buckhorn nodded his chin at Coach. Dawson raised his thermos as he whisked himself up the stairs to his office.

Doug was in his closet-sized office beside the leg extension equipment. Bryce and me walked passed him on the way to the locker room to shower and change.

"How you feeling, Bryce?" Doug said while shuffling papers on his desk.

"Fine," he said.

"Any headaches?"

"What headaches?" Bryce said scratching my scalp.

"I'm fine, Doug, really."

Doug stood and pointed at Bryce. "You're not lying to me, are you?"

Buckhorn emerged behind us. "Checking up on our boys, I see," he said.

"They're supposed to have a day off today," Doug said crossing his arms.

"There's never a day off when you're trying to win a championship, Doug." Patrick winked.

"Did you tell him?" Doug asked Bryce.

"Tell me what?" Patrick eye's zig zagged between the three of us.

"It's nothing, Pat. Honest."

"Did you tell Coach Dawson?"

"What the hell are you talking about?" Patrick asked.

Bryce's eyes pleaded with Doug.

"Talk to Coach Dawson about it." Doug slammed his office door.

"What was that all about?" Patrick asked.

"Nothing. I just got a little light-headed at practice, that's all," Bryce said.

"Should I be concerned?" Patrick asked.

"No," Bryce said.

"Fine. Hit the showers. Good job today. Coop, I want to talk to you for a moment."

Bryce went to the locker room while Patrick pulled me aside by the water fountain, his broad shoulders looming over mine. "You two wouldn't be hiding anything from me, would you?"

"I don't know what you're talking about," I said shaking my head.

"If there's something wrong with Bryce I want to know about it."

"You know as much as I do," I said shrugging my shoulders.

"No bullshit?"

"No bullshit," I replied.

"If this is going to work it's important we be completely honest with each other. Without honesty, the whole damn system breaks down."

I nodded with a weak grin and took a sip from the water fountain. "I'm going to go take a shower."

The locker room smelled of BO and shit, but what locker room doesn't? Bryce was by his locker changing into his jeans. His hair was still wet from the quick shower he'd taken.

"Headaches?"

Bryce, quiet, put on his polo shirt and sprayed cologne. He ran a comb through his jet-black hair.

"You never told me anything about headaches," I pressed.

"It's not a big deal, Coop."

"Are they bad?"

"From time to time. I just try to ignore it."

"Are you taking anything?"

He ignored the question.

"When did the headaches start?"

"Ever since, well…"

"Have you told Coach Dawson?" I asked.

Bryce slammed the locker. The bang echoed through the room. "Just drop it, Coop. And you better not tell anyone else about it either," he said sternly.

I took a shower and changed and walked back out into the hallway. I turned down the hall and found Dawn walking towards me. "Coop! Have you seen Bryce? He told me he would be here, " Dawn said.

"You just missed him. He should still be around."

"Oh," she said, disappointed.

"Everything alright?" I asked.

"Yes, I mean, I suppose. It's just, Bryce's been sort of distant lately. We don't see each other as much."

"He's got a lot on his mind. Give him time."

"Has he said anything to you?"

"About what?"

"Oh, forget it. I shouldn't be asking you that. Beside, you're his friend. You wouldn't tell me anything anyway, even if he talked to you about me."

"Bryce likes you, that's for sure."

"He doesn't show it sometimes," Dawn responded.

"Guys are a pain in the ass, Dawn. Especially ball players. You'll have to get used to that."

Buckhorn, out of his gym clothes and into his business casual attire, found Dawn and I speaking in the hallway. "Dawn, is it?" Buckhorn asked.

"Hi Mr. Buckhorn."

"I hope I wasn't interrupting something."

"No, actually I was looking for Bryce.

Patrick rubbed his chin and crossed his arms, his veins bulging out of his forearms. "You were with Bryce last, weren't you?" Patrick said.

"Bryce left a few minutes ago."

"Oh. He shouldn't be far. Why don't I help you find him?" Patrick offered to Dawn.

"Sure! Coop, you coming?"

"I have class in ten minutes."

"Oh, well. I'll be see you later then," she replied.

The exit was straight ahead. I made my way out, leaving Buckhorn and Dawn alone. Dawn let out an obnoxious laugh as I left.

Practice ended an hour early that day. Bryce and I remained on the field. Buckhorn wasn't around, forced to attend a fundraising event with some alumni. It was a relief.

The team had a great day of practice. We were in first place and running on all cylinders. Bryce was on a tear, leading the league in hitting, despite his migraines, which he wouldn't talk about.

You couldn't tell anything was wrong from the way he played. He still made it look easy, and that annoyed the hell out of me.

I had to work twice as hard to be competitive.

Bryce and I threw in the outfield. I didn't have time to throw much during practice and I needed to make up for it. My arm felt great. Not ninety miles per hour great, but still, I was winning. We were winning. As long as it stayed that way, the secrets were manageable.

"So how are things with Alison?"

The ball rolled off my fingers as I fired a fastball at close range. Bryce grimaced and shook his catching hand from the sting of the ball popping the mitt.

"Easy, buddy, let me back up first," Bryce said, furthering the distance between us.

I grinned, not listening to his requests. I whipped my arm through the air, firing one fastball after another, hoping to sting his catching hand again.

I threw some curveballs and a sweet changeup.

"Me likey," Bryce said. He got up and took off his mask. "Let's call it a day. My legs are killing me."

The dugout was riddled with sunflower seed shells that crunched with every step of our cleats. "I feel like an old man. I'm sore everywhere," Bryce said.

"We got a day off Monday. You should rest."

"We got that weight room session with Buckhorn, remember? This time he wants the whole team there. Wants us on a new training regimen."

"Who's the coach, him or Dawson?"

"Dude, I just play here. Besides, Buckhorn has vision. Dawson just wants to keep his job."

"Don't we all?" I said.

Samson and Zach hit at the batting cage beside the field. Zach was behind the netted L-screen throwing BP to Samson. The floor of the cage, littered with baseballs as Samson hit line drive after line drive against the back net of the cage. He hit a line drive right back at the L-screen, nearly knocking Zach over. "Watch it!" Zach yelled.

"Relax, you're behind the L-screen, you pussy."

"Maybe I'll throw one at your head," Zach said with a weak smile, as Bryce and I approached the cage. We leaned over on one of the metal beams that held up the net of the cage. Zach threw a few more pitches out of the strike zone.

Samson became frustrated with Zach's inaccuracy. "Seriously?"

"Relax, will ya? It'll come back to me." Zach reached the strike zone. The cling of the metal bat chimed with distinct authority as Samson hit the ball in the sweet spot. "Why can't you hit like that during the game?" asked Bryce.

"Shut up, I have a three-game hitting streak going."

" You pay too much attention to stats," Bryce replied.

"Every player pays attention to stats. I'm just willing to admit it. Right, Coop?" Samson asked slyly.

Zach tossed a few more pitches before he ran out of balls. We helped Samson and Zach pick up the scattered balls in the cage and tossed them back in the bucket.

"My arm's tired," Zach said.

"Oh come on. I can use a few more cuts!" Samson exclaimed.

"Hey buddy I need some batting practice too. Bryce can pitch," Zach said.

"Nah. I'm sore. Let Coop pitch. He could get some more work in," Bryce suggested.

Zach balked at the idea. "That's OK. Besides, Coop's arm could use the rest. He needs it."

"I'm fine. I need the work."

"It's not necessary."

"Really, it's no big deal."

"I said no, Coop."

I flexed my chest. My face burned as I argued with him.

"You're making too much of a big deal over this, Coop. Just let it go," Zach said, rolling his eyes.

I grabbed the net and shook it, knocking over some balls that sat on top of it. "I just want to know why you don't want me pitching to you."

"I told you. We need you for our game against St. Leo."

"Bullshit," I said throwing my glove at the ground, creating billow of dust that hovered over to the cage.

"Come on, Zach. Why don't you just be honest with him?" Samson said tossing a ball in his hand.

"I don't know what you're talking about," Zach said, looking the other way.

"Come on. I think we all know what this is about," Samson said.

"Why don't you enlighten us, Samson?" I said.

"Would all of you shut up?" Bryce yelled.

"Oh, come on, Bryce. Of all people you should see it's blatantly obvious," Samson motioned to Bryce. "What's that?" Bryce asked.

"Zach here doesn't want to get beamed in the face."

I threw the gate of the cage open and lunged at Samson, tackling him to the ground. We rolled around the floor as Bryce and Zach tried to break us apart. I rolled Samson over and pinned him on the ground like a wrestler.

"Get off, asshole!" Samson yelled.

Bryce lifted me off the ground and held me back against the net. Zach helped Samson up. Zach had to wrap his arms around Samson to hold him back.

"It was just a joke!" Samson yelled.

"Some joke."

"Screw you, Coop." In the corner of my eye I saw someone watching us. When I looked I spotted Miguel hiding behind a lamppost in front of a family of trees that resided behind the field. When Miguel realized that I'd noticed him, he walked off and disappeared into the brush.

"What is it?" Bryce asked, seeing my distraction.

"Nothing."

Zach pulled Samson to the back of the cage so he could cool off. "What the hell is his problem?" I asked Bryce.

"Don't know. Maybe some people just don't like each other for whatever reason. Human nature, I suppose."

Samson picked up his gear and gave me a disgusted look before he left the cage.

"The kid's got an odd sense of humor," Zach said.

"No shit," I said.

"You think he'll tell Coach?"

"Tell what? That he got pinned by the pitcher for being a smartass? Nah."

"I'll talk to him," said Bryce. "The kid listens to me, for whatever reason. I think it's because I helped him get laid freshman year with that History major."

"A real humanitarian," Zach joked.

On the way back to campus I stopped at The Grind, a student favorite for those who wanted a strong cup of coffee for those late night study sessions. I felt drained and I needed some caffeine to get homework done for the evening. Zach walked in a few minutes after me. "I'm buying," he said.

"You don't have to do that," I said.

"Just for all the trouble."

"We can thank Samson for that."

"Samson is like a child. He has no filter. He blurts out whatever comes to mind. The kid isn't a mental heavyweight like you, Coop. You let him get the best of you."

"I wasn't in the mood."

I ordered a large coffee from the pink-haired barista while Zach ordered one of those exotic Frappuccinos with enough sugar to give the entire campus diabetes. "How can you drink that?" I asked.

"Everything in moderation, Coop."

Soft jazz played in the background. A few students sat at the table across from us with their laptops on full display. The hissing sound of the espresso machine run by a longhaired, bearded hipster drowned out the jazz music and anyone trying to have an actual conversation.

Zach loved going to coffee houses and poetry readings in his spare time. Kind of odd tastes for a ball player, I thought. The Grind was his scene. He often went there to study and just relax. I couldn't understand how he could do either with that damned espresso machine wailing like a freight train.

"I checked the standings. We're in first with a three-game lead over Georgia. Not too shabby," Zach said.

"No, not too shabby at all," I replied.

"Soon you'll get picked up by the pros, with the way you're pitching."

I took a long sip of coffee "Maybe," I said. "You're having a good season yourself. I'm sure a few scouts have taken a good look at you. You're fifth in the league in hitting, for crying out loud."

"I've been offered a minor league contract. I turned it down," Zach said.

I nearly spit my coffee. "You turned down a minor league contract!? Why on Earth did you do that?" I asked.

"Are you kidding? Spending the next five to ten years of my life with a bunch of knuckleheads like the ones I play with on a daily basis? No offense."

"None taken. But what about the money? The pros?"

"That crossed my mind. I never said it wasn't tempting. But if there is one thing I've learned, it's that you shouldn't do something just for the money. Besides, I want to travel a bit. See the world. Maybe join the Peace Corps or something. After I sow my royal oats I might give the bigs a shot. I mean, we're young right? The whole world is waiting for us. At least that's what they keep telling us," Zach said.

"You're an oddball, Zach," I said.

"Maybe you're right. This damn Frappuccino is too sweet." White strands of sugar swirled in the creamy concoction. He grimaced after taking another sip. "The meeting is going to happen soon."

"Meeting?"

"You remember what we talked about, don't you? You didn't think I forgot?"

I looked at him. Those dark, scrunched eyes bored into me, and I saw something seething behind them..

"And I suppose you will be the judge?"

"I *am* Pre-Law. Look at it like an informal trial."

"Why are you doing this, Zach?"

"Because it's the right thing to do, that's all. We owe it to the team. We owe it to Bryce. Don't you think?"

"I don't owe anybody anything."

"Oh," Zach said, disapprovingly.

"I don't care about this damn fraud of a trial. I got nothing to hide."

"Then you have nothing to worry about," replied Zach.

"Who said I was worrying?"

"You seem worried."

"Maybe I just won't go," I said.

"Sure. But what happened shook up a lot of the guys last year. Believe it or not, your reputation is on the line. If you don't do this, you'll make things worse for yourself. You're a captain now. It's a big deal." He swirled his cup with such nonchalance. "We're all going to graduate soon. And when we get out into the world, we'll carry with us what happened that day, and how you went about it. That day I saw you at the hospital; you didn't seem to show remorse. I want to make sure I'm wrong about you."

Zach threw out his unfinished drink and got a cup of regular coffee instead. He started towards the door before he turned to me.

"Should I have been worried today?" he asked.

"About?"

"You hitting me in the cage."

"You had nothing to worry about, Zach," I said with a weak smile.

"Right." He nodded.

I stayed a while and watched the baristas craft various drinks. I didn't want to go back to my dorm. I didn't want to run into Zach or Bryce. Frankly, I had no interest in seeing anybody.

# Chapter 14

Sunday evening I sat in the dining hall staring down a dry chicken breast smothered in questionable marsala sauce. When I bit into the chicken, it felt like I was chewing a rubber tire. I washed it down with a swig from my carton of milk, amusing myself by watching a student across from me pick his nose.

Bryce wandered into the hall as if he were searching for his lost dog. He came to me with bloodshot eyes and a flushed face.

"What's the matter with you? "I asked.

I'd never seen Bryce this emotional before. He wasn't the sobbing type. Yet, here he was, an emotional basket case.

"It's Dawn," he said.

"You guys having problems?".

"We got into an argument," he said.

"About what?"

Bryce looked exhausted. I hadn't seen him outside of Brass Field for the past few days. He looked like he lost weight. I'd never seen Bryce like this before. There was an odd sensation of pleasure that washed over me, seeing him in that condition. I'm not sure how much of the empathetic side of me was left.

"I broke up with Dawn," he said.

"What? Why?"

A few tears dripped down his face. He wiped them away and covered his face with one hand when someone walked by. "I liked this one, Coop. I really did. I think I fell for her."

"Then why the hell did you break up with her, you idiot?"

"Buckhorn told me to."

"What!?"

"He told me he ran into Dawn at the gym. Said she was becoming too much of a distraction, especially when I start my professional career."

"And you believed all that crap?"

"We need this championship, Coop. You know how important it is for the school. But, I mean, I love Dawn." Bryce pressed the palm of his hands against his face. He was in complete agony. "What am I going to do?"

"Why did you listen to Buckhorn?"

"He's the reason I got the contract with the Pirates, Coop. He's my mentor. Pat knows about these things. He's been there."

"He's just some damn Athletic Director, Bryce. And you're letting him run your life!"

"It was my decision."

"Was it?" I said.

"What do you know? You're not the one going to the show. I am. It's a lot of pressure. This team needs me. And the last thing I need is people second guessing me and playing with my mind."

"And what do you think Buckhorn's doing? You're just too blind to see it."

Bryce took a piece of my bread stick and devoured it.

"When was the last time you ate? " I asked.

"This morning. I had a protein bar."

"You should eat something," I said.

"Maybe later. What the hell should I do, Coop?" he asked.

I dropped my fork on the bland plate of chicken and cracked my knuckles. Bryce hated when I did that. "Simple. You get Dawn back."

He fidgeted in his chair and gazed at me with bloodshot eyes. "How?"

"Tell her you were confused. You weren't thinking straight. That you realized you'd fallen in love with her and you got scared. "

Bryce leaned over the table. "Will it work?"

I shrugged. "It's worth a shot. Better than feeling sorry for yourself."

Bryce's eyes widened "Could Alison talk to her?"

"Alison?"

"Yeah! They're friends, right? Maybe she could patch things up with Dawn. Smooth things over before I talk to her," he said.

"I don't know," I said.

"Why?" Bryce asked, inching forward on the table.

"Alison, she's a complicated girl, Bryce. Considering you broke up with Dawn, she might encourage her not get back with you. She's cynical that way."

"Alison wouldn't do that! Maybe I should talk with her," Bryce said lifting himself off the chair before I grabbed his hand.

"Not a good idea," I said before Bryce sat back down on the chair.

He thought to himself for a moment before his face lit up with hope. "*You* talk to Dawn," Bryce said.

"Who, me?" I asked.

"Of course. Why didn't I think of that before? Dawn's always raved about how nice and smart you are. She'll listen to you."

"I can't."

"Sure you can. We're best friends, Dawn knows that. That's why she'll listen to you. She knows you understand me better than anybody!"

"You're the one that should be talking to her. Not me."

"Please, Coop. I can't bring myself to talk to her right now. I'm a fucking mess. This would mean a lot to me."

Helping Bryce was comical. I enjoyed watching him suffer. I don't know, maybe I should have felt sorry for him. And for a moment, I did. But I hated him for different reasons now. No longer was it because he was superior, but because I was beginning to become superior to him. He was pathetic, like a child who lost his toy. I looked for excuses to hate him, and I realized that he was taking away the very thing that had kept me going all this time. My mediocrity.

I needed something to fill the void. So I played along. I would pretend to be his friend. I would pretend to be his trustworthy confidante in his moment of crisis. And when the time came, I would make him understand the pain I felt living in his shadow.

"Fine. I'll talk to her," I sighed.

"Seriously?"

" Yes," I said, tapping my finger on the cafeteria table.

"I appreciate this, bud. When do you plan on talking to her?"

"Can I at least finish my dinner first?"

"Right!" He laughed. "I don't want to rush you or anything. I mean, it's just, the longer we wait, well, the less likely she'll want to get back with me."

"I'll talk with her tomorrow."

"Thanks, Coop!"

"Don't thank me. I haven't done anything yet. Besides, we don't know how she'll even react."

"Of course," Bryce said.

"Just do nothing stupid, like stalk her or call her twenty times and leave her psychotic voicemails."

Bryce agreed with a nervous laugh.

"You're going to do *what*?" Alison asked, stunned. "That's the stupidest thing I've ever heard."

"Why is it stupid?" I asked.

"Because Bryce is the one who broke up with her. He's the one that should talk to her, not you."

"He's just been confused. He didn't really want to break up with her."

"That makes no sense. He needs to grow up," Alison said shaking her head.

"Look, there's a lot more to this than meets the eye."

"How so?"

"Are you going to help me with this or not?" I pleaded.

Alison was working at the college bookstore next to The Grind. A tall, lanky blond-haired kid with freckles and a Tampa State T-shirt that screamed freshman strolled in. He asked Alison with his high-pitched voice if they stocked *Latin America in the 21ˢᵗ Century* by Hugh Vincent.

"Did you check the History section?" Alison asked.

"No, but it's not a History class. I'm studying Latin American Affairs and it ain't there either," he said with a cracked voice.

Alison huffed and checked the computer. "It says we have one."

"Can you help me find it?" Asked the freshman.

Alison rolled her eyes and led the freshman through the aisles of the bookstore. She swore she'd seen it between Calculus and Biology.

"Ahha," she exclaimed. She pulled out the book from the bottom shelf in the English section. "I've told Matt a thousand times to stock these books correctly. God!" Alison said to herself. "Anything else I can help you find?"

"This is last year's edition. I need this year's," the freshman said.

"There's no difference between last year's and this year's addition, hun. The book manufacturers are just trying to screw you out of money. They keep printing the same book stamping edition one hundred or whatever on the cover. Besides, buying the older additions is cheaper. Trust me, I'm doing you a favor."

The freshman was convinced. She rang him up and shoved the book into a plastic bag. "Older editions. Remember that."

"Thanks!" Said the freshman who tried to shake Alison's hand. She grabbed it by the finger and shook it up and down to the freshman's confusion.

"Lord," Alison said. "I can't even remember when I was a freshman." Said said as her nose crinkled.

"Can we get to the task at hand?" I said waving my hands in front of her face.

"Oh, right. Listen, I still think you shouldn't be talking to her for him. It's his responsibility."

"Ok, so why don't you talk to her?"

"Me?" The corner of her mouth quirked up.

"Yeah, you're her friend right?"

"I mean, I suppose. We met up for coffee and went shopping a few times. But I wouldn't say we were best buds. She's sort of odd, to tell you the truth. Doesn't say much. Always talks about knitting, for whatever reason. I don't know what Bryce sees in her. Still, I don't know why he can't talk to her."

"Look, I shouldn't be saying this. Bryce broke up with her because Buckhorn told him to."

"Told him to?"

"Yes. He thinks Dawn will just distract him and hold him back when he reaches the pros. The guy is a megalomaniac. He's just pushing us so we can win a championship so the school can get lucrative donations. He looks at us as pawns in his little game."

"Oh come on, that's ridiculous," She said shaking her head and rolling her eyes.

"It's the truth."

"Well, shame on Bryce for not acting like a grown man and making his own damn decisions."

"We're under a lot of pressure, Alison. You've never played college sports before. They want results. No winning, no spot on the team. No scholarship means no school. Or you take out a student loan and get into a boat-load of debt."

"You boys and your sports," Alison said. "And I don't see how Buckhorn is a megalomaniac? He spoke very highly of you yesterday," She said creating a stack of calculus books on the cart beside her.

"Yesterday?" I said cocking my head.

"Yeah, I talked to him for a good forty five minutes while I was on the treadmill. He seems to think you have a lot of potential."

"Don't talk to him anymore," I said crossing my arms.

"What? Why?"

"Because he's not who you think he is," I said.

"Oh, you're just being ridiculous. I think being out in the sun all day is rotting your brain," Alison said while organizing some books from a nearby bookshelf.

"You never take what I say seriously," I said, squinting.

Alison pinched my cheek and gave me a peck on the lips. "I do take you seriously. You are just wound up like a tinker toy, hun."

She ran her hand through my hair, soothing me like you could never imagine.

"When do you plan on speaking with Dawn?" she asked.

"Tonight. I've tried calling her several times but I haven't been able to reach her. I plan on stopping by her dorm and ask if she wants to get coffee."

"What will you say to her?"

"That's the thing. I don't know. That's why I need your help."

"Good Lord, it's a miracle you were able to get in my pants," Alison said with a wide grin.

"Thanks for the confidence boost."

"Just be honest with her. Tell her how Bryce feels about her and what he's going through. Though I wouldn't mention Buckhorn. That makes Bryce look pathetic. Does he love her?"

"Yeah."

Alison bit her bottom lip, in deep thought. "Hmm, well, I don't know if you should tell her he loves her. Bryce should tell her that himself. Focus on getting her to meet with him. Ease the tension between the two, then just let the pieces fall as they may."

"That's it?" I asked.

"Women may be complicated, but sincerity sure helps."

"I'll remember that."

I left Alison re-stocking empty shelves with Bryce calling me every few minutes. I called him back. He told me to meet him in front of Brass Field, as he was going for an evening run just so he could get his mind off of things.

The gnats around the field were annoying. They kept buzzing my ear with extreme prejudice. I kept swatting them away, but they kept coming. Bryce sprinted the last several hundred feet until he reached me at the main gate. He was drenched in sweat. His hair was wet and oily, as if he'd just got out of the shower. He sure as hell could've used one. "Did you talk to her?" he asked, jogging in place as he spoke.

"No. I told you. I called her several times. No luck. How about you?"

"Nothing," Bryce said with a frown. Now doing some leg stretches. "You're going over to her dorm, right? You know where it is?"

"Yes, I know where it is. You told me five times. It's Cabot Hall, right near the science building. She probably isn't even there."

"It's Wednesday night. She'll be there. She has Calculus Thursday mornings. She's usually studying in her dorm. Do you know what you will say to her?"

"I have a few ideas."

"And?"

"And what?" I said with a deadpan look.

"What are they?" Bryce said, shaking my shoulders.

"Don't you trust me?"

"I want to know what you're going to tell her."

"I will tell her you're a great guy and you were just confused."

"That's it?"

"I'm ad libbing, but something like that."

"Aren't you going to tell her how I feel?"

"Shouldn't you be telling Dawn that yourself?"

"Are you kidding? She hates my guts right now. She won't listen to a word I say. When you smooth things over with her, then I'll tell her. But I still want her to know how much she means to me. In a somewhat discreet way."

"You're giving me second thoughts," I said with a raised eyebrow.

"Okay, okay. Use your best judgment," Bryce said.

"Alright then. But I want to reiterate that I'm not making any promises."

"What do you think she'll say, Coop?" Bryce asked, concerned.

"Well, there are several scenarios. One is that she breaks down in tears because of your affection for her and I'm a damn good salesman. Second scenario is that she becomes even more confused. Third, she becomes angry and resents you, destroying any chance of you two getting back together."

"Could she be *that* angry at me?"

"I don't know, buddy. Women hold all the cards, bud. It's just the hand we're dealt."

"Please help me, Coop," Bryce begged. "I don't know what else to do."

I put my hand on his shoulder and peppered him with some encouragement. "Look, everything will be fine. I'm sure Dawn will understand. At the very least, I'm sure she'll want to see you again. You trust me?" I said, biting my tongue, laughing on the inside.

Bryce nodded his head in agreement.

"That settles it. I'll call you when I leave her dorm. Where will you be?"

"Back at the dorm."

"Will do," I said.

The campus shuttle service had ended for the evening, but I didn't mind the thirty minute walk to Cabot Hall. The mixture of oak and palm trees and lush grass from the quads and open spaces in between the academic and administrative buildings made it a pleasant stroll. Students walked or rode on bikes or skateboards, zig-zagging through the various nooks and crannies of campus.

Cabot Hall is one of Tampa State's original buildings dating back to 1940, serving as barracks for the soldiers training there during WWII. It was a three-storey rectangular brick building with steel-framed windows. Cabot Hall was etched in a stone slab above the red doors of the main entrance. The door creaked open. The smell of must hit my nostrils.

A stairway and a curly-haired hall monitor reading a textbook while jotting on a notepad, greeted me at the main entrance. Either she didn't see me, or couldn't have cared less. The dorm wasn't co-ed, and although it was common to see a member of the opposite sex roam the grounds of Cabot, I still didn't want to risk stirring things up. I tiptoed past the curly-haired girl at her desk and sneaked my way up the stairs to Dawn's third floor dorm, the last room to the right. The hallways were dimly lit. Cabot wasn't fully occupied. Many of the students opted for off-campus housing rather than stay in what could be considered closets with beds stashed in them.

Most of the dorm doors were closed. The few that were open showed girls just minding their own business. The environment felt sterile and colorless. The white walls and brown tile that decorated the halls made me feel I was in a time warp. No wonder students didn't want to stay there. The third floor was just a void. Some punk music was blaring from the dorm room to my immediate left. The drone of the music followed me as I walked down the hall.

I made my way towards the door when I noticed a slither of amber light pierce through the crease of Dawn's dorm room illuminating the tiled white hallway. I heard a commotion coming from inside. She wasn't alone. I debated whether to leave and come back at a better time.

But I kept walking towards the door. I began to push the door open when I noticed Dawn standing naked in her underwear. The bed wasn't visible from my point of view unless I pushed the door open a bit further. Dawn got on top of the bed.

I couldn't see his face at first. I knew for sure it wasn't Bryce. He wouldn't have bothered to make such a fuss about me talking to Dawn if that were the case. Also, the man lying in Dawn's bed was bigger than Bryce. I tried to get a good look at his face before I saw a Tampa State polo slung over Dawn's desk chair. Moans of ecstasy intertwined with the punk music playing down the hall, creating an ambiance of lust and a primitive rawness

His hands glided down her back as she moaned in approval. I had to see who it was. But if I pushed open the door any further the gig was up. Dawn repositioned herself. In the midst of her repositioning, I saw his face. His white teeth gleamed with delight as Dawn pleasured him. The moment seemed surreal. Yet, there it was, before my eyes. Buckhorn and Bryce's girl. Another secret.

I heard someone come down the hall. Buckhorn briefly drew his attention towards the door. Our eyes locked. I clenched my teeth in fear.

"Hey, what are you doing?" the girl asked from down the hall, wrapped in a wet towel. I sprinted down the hall, nearly knocking her over. She held onto my windbreaker but I broke free and didn't look back. I don't know if Buckhorn got a good look at me.

I heard a door slam open as I ran down the stairs. "Who was that?"

"I don't know." The voices fell distant as I bolted through the main entrance.

"Slow down!" the curly-haired girl said.

I ran as hard as I could, not caring which direction I went. I ran until Cabot Hall was no longer visible. I stopped to catch my breath. I checked to see if Buckhorn was behind me, or campus security, even. I wandered around for a few minutes until I regained my composure. I checked to see if campus security had been called.

I waited fifteen minutes. Nothing. I sat by a nearby bench for a few minutes until I could catch my breath. After ten minutes I went to the dining hall. All my meal card could afford was a few donuts and chocolate milk.

I took my time, not wanting to go back to the dorm and face Bryce. I felt my phone vibrate in my pocket. Six missed calls from Bryce. I watched TV to distract myself. The phone continued ringing. I turned it off so I could get my head straight. *What do I tell him?* Repeated in my mind over and over.

There was always the truth. But the truth was messy. People preferred comfortable lies over the hard truth with pretty much everything. I worried that Bryce might go over to Dawn's dorm himself. *Would he catch them there?* He was capable of doing anything at this point.

I hurried back to the dorm. On the way to Orsini Hall I found Miguel, in jeans and a ruffled-up polo, sitting at the park bench eating a sandwich straight out of the wrapper. He saw me, dropped his sandwich, and ran in the other direction. It might have been comical to an outside observer. I chased him down. This time, he wouldn't get away. I tackled him to the ground. He tried to crawl away, but I pinned him with my knee.

"Let go of me!" Miguel yelled.

"Why are you running away? I want to talk to you!" I said.

"Get off of me, you jerk," Miguel yelled.

"I will if you stop running away! You promise?"

"Fine, you dick, just get off."

I lifted myself off Miguel, but stayed close in case he tried to run away again. He dusted himself off and fixed his hair. "You were always faster than me, Coop."

"Why have you been following me?" I asked.

"Following you?"

"I saw you by the field last week."

"Yes. You and Samson aren't playing nice."

"Quit dicking around. Why are you following me?"

"I'm checking up on my pal. Look at me as your guardian angel," he said with a snicker. "Besides, I like visiting campus. Reminds me of the good ol' days."

"Then why were you running away?"

"We're all running away from something," he sneered. "You should know, Coop."

I grabbed him by the collar. "Shut up."

"Hey, can I crash in your dorm tonight? I'm exhausted," he said. I released him from my grip.

"You're fucking crazy."

"Tut tut, Coop. That's no way to talk to a friend." He fidgeted in between sentences. "But, if you insist, I'll go."

Miguel picked up his sandwich he'd dropped near the steel bench and continued eating it as he walked away.

I dashed up to my dorm room. I found Bryce there pacing back and forth.

"Where the hell were you?" he yelled. "I called you ten times!"

"Sorry," I said, shutting the door behind me.

"You were supposed to have called me when you left. What happened?" Bryce asked desperately.

"Sorry. My phone died. I ate something afterward. I would've invited you but my phone needed a charge."

Bryce relaxed as he saw the logic in my excuse. "Fine. So tell me, what happened? What did she say? And why do you look like you just got in a fight?" Bryce had noticed the grass and dirt stains on the windbreaker from my tussle with Miguel.

"Oh, I haven't had a chance to change. That reminds me, I have to do laundry."

"Sure. Do that. Now, would you finally tell me what she said?" Bryce pleaded.

The truth lay on the tip of my tongue. I took off my windbreaker, leaving him in suspense. I sort of enjoyed it. It gave me power over him. Power I hadn't felt in a long time. I wanted to play with him. I became his puppet master. My lies were the strings that played with his mind.

"It went well," I said, with my back turned to him as I stuffed my windbreaker into the hamper beside the closet.

"Really?" he asked ecstatically. "What happened? Tell me every detail!"

"There isn't a whole lot to tell. I told her how you felt about her. How you were just under a lot of stress and you didn't want her to feel the strain of all the pressure you've been under. But that you realized how wrong you were and that you needed her in more ways than she knew," I said, holding back a grin.

"Did you tell her I loved her?"

"Nah. I would've come off as cheesy. Besides, that's something *you* gotta tell her."

"So she said she'll get back with me?"

"She didn't say that. But she did get teary-eyed, I must admit. She certainly still has feelings for you. I loaded up the base pads for you, buddy. Now it's your turn at the plate. You gotta bring 'em home."

Bryce jumped for joy and rushed over to hug me. It was awkward, but I played along, patting him on the back like a brother.

"Thanks, Coop. I owe you one," Bryce said.

"Don't mention it." He changed into a new pair of jeans and began rifling through his closet. "What are you doing?"

"I'm going to change. Dawn can't look at me like this." He sniffed underneath his armpits. "I should probably shower, don't you think?"

My brain raced with the words or phrases I could use to convince him not to leave.

"You can't see her now!" I spat.

"Why the hell not?"

"Not tonight. She said she was going to bed after I left because of a big calculus exam tomorrow and she wanted to rest."

"It's still early," Bryce replied. "I'll call her."

"No. Don't do that."

"If she wants to see me I'm sure she won't mind if I just give her a call."

"Come on, Bryce. After all the women you've been with, you're acting like a damn virgin freshman. Listen, you got to play a little hard to get. Don't make it so easy for her. Girls like a challenge."

He sighed in frustration and collapsed on the bed, rubbing his face. "When?"

"You ever heard of the two day rule?"

"That's so 1990s, Coop," Bryce scoffed.

"It still works," I said.

"Look, first thing tomorrow I'm going to see her. I'm laying it all out for her." Bryce stopped himself for a moment and laughed. "Funny. I never thought I would get all worked up over a girl like this."

"It happens," I said. "But one other thing – Don't mention that I talked to her tonight."

"What? Why?" he asked.

"Because she thinks I spoke to her on my own initiative. If she found out you asked me to speak to her it will ruin the whole thing. Pretend I never spoke to her. Just go up to her and spill your heart out. She'll see not only what a great guy you are, but what a wonderful friend I am. She'll tell Alison how lucky she is to have a guy like me. It's a win-win."

I was wondering if I was having delusions of grandeur, thinking my lie would somehow work, especially if Dawn told him the truth about her and Buckhorn. But seeing Bryce become this smaller, weaker version of his former self left me in awe as to how one can change so quickly, all due to the slightest external change. He was my little experiment in the realm of the human psyche.

Bryce was upbeat again. He even wanted to go for a late-night run. I declined because I was tired. I advised him to rest up, as we had a three-game road series against Georgia that weekend and he needed all his strength, but he was too excited to sleep. He decided to go to the weight room and burn off all his pent up energy. I was glad he left. I wanted to sleep.

The room fell dark as I turned off the light. I tossed and turned in bed that night, unable to sleep. I kept thinking about Buckhorn talking to Alison. That damn grin of his and those white pearly teeth. I clenched the pillow, fighting my way to sleep.

Revulsion swooped over me. The secrets I held beared down on me, stalking me, unrelenting in their determination to take whatever empathy I had left. My mind split into two people: one who gave a shit, another who seemed to enjoy the pain. I felt my sanity begin to slip away.

Little by little, with each passing day, I lost sense of who I was. My old self nothing but a stranger I was no longer fond of. The new me started to emerge. And I was beginning to like it.

# Chapter 15

The Silverbacks squad waited in front of Brass Field for the Greyhound bus that would take us to Georgia. I waited alone, away from the rest of the team, sipping my large coffee from The Grind. I was starting tomorrow, and I wanted my mind clear. The rest of the guys understood that. Samson was goofing around with a few of the other guys. Zach was reading a book as he leaned against his duffel bag. The sky was a pinkish hue as the sun rose to greet us to a new morning.

I hadn't slept the night before. I'd tossed and turned, thinking about what I saw back at Cabot Hall and the lie I told Bryce. I feared it would backfire in the worst way. The coffee helped but I saved the rest so I could sleep on the bus. Coach Dawson, in a Tampa State jogging suit, spoke with a few of the coaches before he found me standing alone by the curb.

"You look tired," he said.

"Didn't sleep much," I replied.

"Get some sleep on the bus. You'll have plenty of time to sleep once we get to the hotel. We need you rested for tomorrow."

"Sure, Coach."

"And what's this buddy-buddy crap going on between you and Buckhorn?"

"I'm not buddy-buddy with him, Coach. I can't speak for Bryce, though. Buckhorn's just been training with us, helping us with a little strength and conditioning," I said.

It pissed him off, but he had no choice but to take it. Buckhorn held all the cards. Dawson's job was on the line, and he would have to play along.

"Now that you mentioned it, where *is* Bryce?"

"I don't know."

"You're his roommate. How do you not now?"

"When I woke up he was gone."

"Gone?"

"Yup."

"He better show up in the next five minutes or else I'm benching his ass. Six a.m. means six a.m.," Dawson stressed.

Other players continued to stream in. Six a.m. was fast approaching and Bryce was nowhere to be seen.

"Where's Bryce?" Zach asked.

"Like I told Dawson, I haven't the slightest idea."

I had my suspicions where he was. My heart raced thinking about what he would find going to Dawn's dorm. If Buckhorn was still there. The game tomorrow had begun not to matter anymore. I wondered if Bryce had discovered the truth. He would know I lied to him.

"He's been pretty down over Dawn. Is he okay?" Zach asked walking towards me with a cup of coffee.

"He'll be fine," I said.

"You don't sound sure."

"What do you want from me? He's a big boy, he can take care of himself."

"Easy, Coop. He's my friend too."

"Yes, Zach."

"Alright then. I hope he shows up soon or his ass is getting benched. We need him for this series," Zach tossing a baseball at me he grabbed from the pocket of his windbreaker..

The bus rolled up to the curb, screeched and hissed to a halt. It was after six and Bryce was still absent.

"Where's our catcher?" Samson asked obnoxiously loudly, so that everyone could hear.

"He'll be here," I said.

"Sure about that?" Samson asked.

"We'll find out soon enough, won't we," I said, crossing my arms.

We loaded our belongings onto the bus when Bryce, duffel bag and all, sprinted toward us like a madman.

"She said yes!" Bryce said with a goofy smile on his face as he caught his breath.

"Where the hell were you? Dawson's going to tear you a new one!" I said.

"Dawn and I are back together! Can you believe it! It worked, the whole thing worked. You're a genius!"

"Great. Just get on the bus before Coach finds you."

A booming voice shouted over our noise. It was stern and authoritative and aimed directly at Bryce.

"Bryce! Get your ass over here!" yelled Coach Dawson.

Bryce seemed unfazed. "Hey, Coach. Sorry I'm late."

"Buttercup, do you know what time it is?" asked Dawson.

"I'm sorry, Coach. I, uh, slept in."

"Oh, you slept in? You were supposed to be here by six. It's six thirty. Do you even realize how important this series is against Georgia?"

"I'm sorry, Coach. It won't happen again."

"You're damn right it won't. Because you're out of the lineup tomorrow."

"What!?"

Dawson's eyes lit up with anger. "Son, if you don't lower your voice the only ball you'll be playing is for some rec team in Plant City. You hear me?"

"You can't do this, Coach. You need me tomorrow."

"Oh, well since you think you're in a position to tell me how to coach: two games."

Bryce said nothing, keeping his head down as Dawson got the last word. Out of the corner of my eye I saw Buckhorn emerge from behind me and approach the commotion, which drew the attention of most of the team. Buckhorn was carrying a small suitcase. He clothes were unusually wrinkly and was working a five o'clock shadow.

"What's the meaning of this?" Buckhorn asked.

He noticed most of the team staring at them.

"What the hell are you staring at? On the bus!" Dawson ordered.

I was surprised to see Buckhorn. He never went on any road games with us. Out of the window near the back of the bus I could see Buckhorn and Dawson arguing outside. Bryce sat next to me with a look of embarrassment on his face.

"I let the team down," he said.

"It's just two games. We'll manage," I said. "You're not the only player to get suspended. Hell, look at it as a badge of honor," I said with a weak grin.

"I suppose that's one way to look at it," Bryce replied.

The team looked out the right side of the bus as tempers flared between Buckhorn and Dawson. Dawson kicked the gravel beside his feet and stormed onto the bus. The players immediately sat back in their seats. Dawson took his seat in front of the bus. Buckhorn was the last one to enter before the Greyhound driver closed the doors. Buckhorn looked back and gave us a sly wink. Bryce's goofy smile returned. And all I wanted to do was to get some sleep.

The next day I warmed up in the bullpen before the game. I felt strong, well rested, even with Buckhorn and my secrets looming over me. The game mattered now. I pushed my arm during warm-ups, hoping to hit ninety. Determined to win in spite of the circumstances that swirled around me. I jogged to the dugout. The Georgia sun was hot and unforgiving, the air thick and heavy with humidity. My uniform already drenched with sweat. I noticed Bryce putting on his gear.

"What are you doing?" I asked.

"Eating a pizza. What do you think?" Bryce said.

"I thought you weren't starting?"

"Don't jinx it, Coop. Damn."

I turned to find Buckhorn sitting at the edge of the dugout with his legs crossed and wearing his shades, smiling in our direction. Coach Dawson read the lineup card, stuttering when he mentioned Bryce's name in the starting lineup. Buckhorn had neutered Coach Dawson. This wasn't his team anymore. He was a figurehead. And he knew it.

The game was scoreless through the top of the fourth. Johnnie Reese, our first baseman who played two years for Hillsborough Community College, hit a solo shot to put us up one-nothing. Bryce and I were in sync with the signs. At least for that moment, there was no friction. It was just us and the game. I felt like I pitched twelve innings by the time we reached the top of the fifth.

Bryce was so far hitless, slamming his batting helmet against the helmet shelf when he struck out at his last at-bat. The Georgia pitcher was throwing nothing but gas, hitting the mid to high nineties. I felt my arm tighten as the game progressed. I gave up a double driving in a run to tie the game one apiece at the bottom of the seventh.

"How are you feeling?" Dawson asked.

"Okay." I shrugged, attempting to loosen my shoulder up.

"Can you give me another inning?"

My arm hurt, but I wasn't going to tell him that. "I can, Coach."

Dawson shook his head and thought for a moment.

"What are you thinking, Coach?" Buckhorn asked.

## Wild Pitch

"I'm thinking you should let me coach," Dawson replied.

"You're putting Coop back out there?" Buckhorn asked.

"Yes. I am," Dawson said with a scowl.

"Coop's pitched well. But don't you think you should put a fresh arm out there?"

"I'm fine. It's my call," I said.

"You're pushing your luck, Buckhorn," Dawson said as he went to see the bench coach.

"I just don't want you pushing your arm too hard, Coop," Buckhorn said.

"Oh, I'm touched," I replied.

Buckhorn's weak grin left me irritated as the seventh ended with the game still tied. I left Georgia's batters hitless in the eighth. I gave up a run in the ninth, giving Georgia the lead. I threw my mitt in disgust against the green cement wall of the dugout.

I sat alone at the end of the dugout. My windbreaker covered my right arm. Buckhorn gleamed at me from the other side of the dugout, where he'd watched the game near the hitting circle. Samson hit a double with two outs as the tying run on second. Bryce was the winning run at the plate. He took some practice swings before he approached the right side of the batter's box.

The relief pitcher for Georgia was a side arm pitcher with a quirky delivery that made him difficult to read. Bryce was going 0-4 before the ninth, struggling throughout most of the game. Bryce swung hard for strike one. He stepped out of the batter's box and took a few swings before reentering. He swung again for strike two.

The pitcher got in the stretch, swooped down, his arm nearly touching the dirt beneath him, firing a fastball to the plate. Bryce was caught looking as the pitch hit the catcher's mitt. There was a slight pause before the umpire screamed, "Strike three!"

Moans reverberated through the dugout. Bryce walked back to the dugout and, this time, gently placed his helmet back on the shelf and his bat on the bat rack. Buckhorn patted him on the back and pulled him close, saying a few words that Bryce nodded in agreement to.

The team got an earful from Coach Dawson, who spewed his leftover agitation from today's events. I sat by myself at the end of the dugout with a wet towel over my head, hoping the world would just go away.

―

We stayed at a Howard Johnson's right off the highway, two miles away from the Georgia campus. We were on strict curfew. No one was to leave the hotel. I lay in bed and watched TV while Bryce talked to Dawn on the phone. He acted like a lovesick puppy. It was pathetic. I raised the volume of the TV to deafen me from the mindless drivel.

"Would you turn that down? I'm talking to Dawn," he said, covering his phone with the palm of his hand.

"So go outside," I said, annoyed.

Bryce spoke with her for a few more minutes. "I love you forever," Bryce said before he hung up. I stuck my finger down my throat in response.

"Shut up," Bryce said, throwing his pillow at me.

"'I love you forever' Go fuck yourself," I said.

"Girls like that stuff. It worked this morning. You should have seen her. She even cried! I don't know what you did, but whatever it was, it worked."

"You didn't tell her, did you?"

"Nope. I played dumb. She has no idea."

"Good," I said, somewhat relieved. "Glad you two are back together."

"Thanks. I talked to Buckhorn about it."

I bolted upright in astonishment. "What do you mean, you told him? Why did you do that!"

"It was the right thing to do, Coop. He wasn't upset about it. He was more concerned about my performance today."

Theories drenched my mind like a tsunami. What was Buckhorn going to do now? What was he capable of? Would he continue his affair with Dawn? I enjoyed the deceit of it all, knowing the end result would wound Bryce indefinitely.

"That was a bad idea, Bryce," I said

"What's the big deal?".

"It was none of his business."

"He would have found out anyway."

"Then you could have let him find out on his own. You didn't have to tell him." I threw his pillow back at him. "Sometimes I wonder what's in that brain of yours."

"Sorry," Bryce said with his head down.

He grabbed a complimentary water bottle that was on top of the desk and popped two pills from a bottle he got from his toiletry case.

"Pills?"

"They're for my headaches."

"That bad?"

"I'd prefer not to have them. Especially during a game."

"Did you have them today?"

"What, the headaches?"

"Yes."

"A little. But that's not why I went 0-5. Just a bad day, I guess."

"How many of those you take a day?"

"Twice a day, sometimes. Or just when I have headaches. Geez, you sound like my mother, Coop. They're just pills."

"And I suppose Doug gave them to you, right?"

"Coop, I'm going to take a shower and go to bed. Go to sleep, will ya?" Bryce threw a smaller pillow at me as he entered the bathroom. I chucked it back at the now closed door.

I went over to his toiletry case and found the pill container. *Vicodin* in big black letters covered the face of the bottle. The hiss from the shower stopped. I darted back to bed before he walked into the room, wearing sweatpants and a Tampa State Baseball sweater, drying his hair with a towel.

Bryce closed the blinds, but I could still see the bluish hue from the lights that illuminated the hotel pool.

*Knock knock.*

The sound startled me. Bryce opened it to find Zach in the doorway. "Gentlemen, I hope I'm not intruding."

Zach had a few friends at Georgia who were members of the Kappa Epsilon sorority. The four sisters were downstairs by the pool with Samson, who was showing off his muscles to a busty blonde. She didn't seem very impressed.

"The ladies are eagerly awaiting our arrival, gents," Zach said, peeking through the window shades.

"Are you crazy? What about the coaches and Buckhorn?" I asked.

"I peeked into Coach's room window. He's already asleep. Buckhorn's staying at the Marriott a mile away from here because he doesn't want to stay with us peasants. Besides, all the coaches are staying at the opposite end of the hotel, facing the highway. They won't hear us," Zach said.

Bryce laid in his bed with his hands folded behind his head.

"Don't jump up from all the excitement," Zach said to Bryce. "Aren't you coming?"

"Nah. I'm think I'm staying in. I need some sleep," He said rubbing his eyes.

Zach sat beside Bryce and shook his head. "These aren't just sorority sisters. They are all in the running for the Ms. Georgia beauty pageant! And you're acting like a floppy penis."

"If the man doesn't want to go he doesn't want to go," I said.

Zach stood on the top of the bed and gestured at me like an actor commanding a stage.

"You people are pathetic. I give you women and song and you reject it like I'm beneath you. Let us eat cake, my friends."

Zach jumped and pile drove Bryce, almost knocking him off the bed. Bryce laughed at Zach's enthusiasm and surrendered. "Just a for little while, okay?," Bryce said.

"That's the spirit!" Zach said. "Hurry up and change before Samson scares them off."

"You left Samson alone with them?" I said.

"The kid is a walking erection. What do you want me to do? Hurry up."

Bryce quickly slipped into boxers, and the two of them headed downstairs. I thought about calling Alison, but I knew she would be asleep by now. The chorus of laughter, splashing, and cannonballs wafted into my room. I lay in bed, unable to sleep. The sounds drew me in, intoxicating me with their spell. "Screw it."

I changed into some shorts and quietly made my way downstairs. The night was warm, the heat lingering after a long day of brutal sun.

"Well, look who decided to show up!" Zach said.

Bryce was at the end of the pool talking to a brunette with freckles. Zach was with the blonde that Samson had tried to impress earlier.

"What's he doing here?' Samson asked, annoyed. "Isn't it past your bedtime?"

I kicked a nearby beach ball at him, narrowly missing his head.

"The pool is warm, friend," Zach said.

It was warm. My muscles tingled in relief. I dipped my hair in the water. When I emerged, the brunette was in front of me, wearing a tiny black bikini and examining me with bright blue eyes. "Cooper, right?" she asked.

"Everyone calls me Coop," I said.

"Coop. Nice name," she said.

"What's yours?"

"Kayla."

"So, Kayla, why aren't you all swimming around with the Georgia team?" I asked.

Kayla smiled. "We like being rebels."

"How do you know Zach?"

"He dated Sandra over there." She gestured to the blonde in Zach's arms. Samson was still trying to impress the other two, without much success. They swam around the pool in their swimsuits, leaving Samson alone at the other side of the pool. Zach gazed over at me while Sandra went over to talk to her sorority sisters. I could still feel his hand glide over my chest, and his secret buried in my mind like an anchor, weighing me down along with the rest.

"Zach is a true Renaissance man," I said to Kayla.

"He's sweet. And what about you?"

"What about me?"

"Are you a Renaissance man?"

"I'm an eccentric," I said.

"What's that?"

"I'm just someone with a healthy dose of cynicism," I responded.

"Oh," Kayla said, confused.

"But I'm a sucker for romanticism," I added.

"A romantic, huh? I like that." Kayla smiled.

Sandra splashed water at Kayla, getting her hair wet. "Don't do that, you jerk!"

"Coop, Zach tells me you're a pitcher," Sandra said.

"Starting pitcher."

"Wow, so you must be good."

"Damn good," Bryce added, wading towards us accompanied by the other two sisters.

"Overrated if you ask me," Samson said splashing water in my direction.

"Are you going to play professionally?" Sandra asked.

"I've had a few scouts look at me. No buyers yet. Bryce here got signed by the Pirates."

Sandra's eyes lit up when she heard this. "Really? Wow, you must be really good."

"I'm not bad," Bryce replied. "These guys make me look good. Hell, I was horrible today."

"Right! I was at the game. You didn't hit anything," Sandra said.

"It was an off day," Bryce said, annoyed.

"At least you looked good in your uniform," Michelle, the sorority sister to his right, said with a subtle southern drawl as she wrapped her arm around his.

"Right!" Sandra said, in a valley girl accent.

The night air cooled after midnight. The girls kept us company. I spent time with Kayla alone at the deep end of the pool while the rest of them hung out by the beach chairs next to the barbeque.

"So, I suppose this question is inevitable, but I have to ask. Do you have a girlfriend?" Kayla asked.

"Yes. I mean, well … Sort of?"

"It's a yes or no question."

"It's complicated."

"Oh Lord, like I haven't heard that one before," Kayla said with a roll of her eyes.

"I mean, she doesn't like labels, you know? Thinks it's too cliché."

"And you like that?" Kayla asked.

"It makes things interesting," I said. "But, to uncomplicate things, yeah, you can say she's my girlfriend."

Kayla looked away. "I see."

"Do you have a boyfriend?" I cringed. It sounded so generic and childish, but I had to know.

"I did. We broke up a few months ago. He was a jerk."

"Why was he a jerk?"

"I caught him sleeping with one of my sorority sisters. I would say that makes him a jerk in my book."

"I suppose it does," I said. "You can do better."

"That's sweet," she said, blushing. "It's a shame."

"What is?" I asked.

"That all the good guys are taken." She glanced at me out of the corner of her eye.

"Well, not everyone is who they seem to be."

"What does that mean?"

"Forget it. The cynic in me, I guess."

"I prefer the romantic in you."

"You girls are all the same," I said.

"In what way?"

"You have this idealized view of romance. Maybe it's not all it's cracked up to be."

"You think you have things figured out, huh?"

"It's just an opinion. Opinions are a dime a dozen."

Kayla twisted my chin. "You talk too much."

She slowly leaned over to me, her lips so close to mine. The temptation was all too real. Her blue eyes and red lips were seductive and wanting. I gently pulled myself back from her. She grinned with her head down in embarrassment. "Sorry," Kayla said.

"That's okay."

"You must really like this girl."

"I just don't think it would be good to complicate things any more than they are already," I said.

"You really do talk too much," Kayla said.

Suddenly, a splash of water drenched us from Samson's naked cannonball. Seeing Samson without any clothes was an unwelcome sight.

"Right! Samson has the idea," Sandra said. She slid off her panties and bra and jumped in the pool. The rest of the sisters followed, exposing every inch of their skin, tan lines and all. Bryce dove in with his shorts on. "Party foul!" Sandra said.

"Hey, it's cold," Bryce said. "Zach, jump in!"

"I'm going to the vending machine to get a coke. Would any of you like anything?"

"Whiskey sour!" Sandra yelled.

"Water will have to do, hun." Zach exited through the lobby doors to his right. Not even a minute passed before he darted back through the doors in sheer panic. "Guys. It's Dawson. He's coming!"

"He's not even in the pool yet." Bryce joked.

"Stop joking, you idiot. He'll be here any second. If he finds us here, we're screwed. Come on!"

I lifted Kayla out of the pool. The girls ran to get their clothes.

"No time for that," Zach said.

"We're naked!" Sandra said.

"Your car is right there," Zach said pointing at the parking lot. "Get out of here. I'll call you," Zach said.

The girls scrambled through the white fence that separated the pool area and the parking lot, their hands covering as much as they could. We grabbed our clothes and ran to the door leading to the stairwell, just as Coach Dawson stormed out of the lobby doors in his PJs. We peeked around the edge of the steel door, watching as Dawson searched the pool area like a guard dog on the trail of an intruder. The girls sped off in Kayla's four-door sedan, screeching off into the distance with EDM music blaring from its speakers. Dawson turned toward the sound, watched as the car faded away, and turned to go back inside..

"You think he suspects something?" Samson asked.

"Shit! The girls' bikinis!"

"Why did you tell them to leave their clothes?" I asked Zach.

"Because it's hilarious."

With a puzzled expression, Dawson picked up a pair of wet,

bottoms that lay on the cement floor. He took one last look before he left, infuriated, slamming the lobby door shut.

"Ha! He took them!" Samson joked. "Someone's jerking off with them," He said with a fist pump.

"Gentlemen," Zach said, "I think we've had enough fun for one evening. We better head back. And for Pete's sake, Samson, put your clothes on."

# Chapter 16

We lost the series against Georgia that weekend. Coach Dawson was furious, but there was only so much he could do while Buckhorn was watching.

The bus ride home was a quiet one. Most of the players slept with DJ sized headphones over their baseballs caps. Bryce had bags of ice on his sore knees and slept for most of the drive back to Tampa. Dawson didn't say a word to us once we arrived back home, except to tell us to go home and get some rest. We needed it.

I'd thought I surprise Alison by stopping by her dorm when we got back. I didn't talk to her much during the trip, just a quick phone call when we first arrived and a text here and there. It was late Sunday evening, but I'd figured she'd still be awake.

I went up the stairs to find her door open. I heard a strange noise coming from inside. I knocked, apprehension clutching my throat. "Come in!" a high pitched voice called.

When I opened the door I was relieved to find Alison, Joanna, and Dawn sitting Indian-style in front of the tiny TV watching a chick flick. "Hey!" Alison said. "You're back."

She leaped up, hugged me and pecked me on the cheek. Joanna

glared at me with annoyance. Dawn seemed indifferent, still sucked into the movie.

"We decided to have a girls' night while you boys were away," Alison said.

"Looks like you're having fun."

"We *were*," Joanna said rolling her eyes.

"I should go. I just wanted to see you before I went back to my dorm."

"No, don't go, silly. I was about to make a coffee run anyway. You can come with me."

The campus was quiet, even for a Sunday. We took our time as we strolled to The Grind, kissing and holding hands, occasionally grazing my fingers around her lower back, feeling the tiny hairs on her back stand from the touch of my hand.

"So, I was talking to Dawn."

I got nervous, foreign to the secret world of girl talk where anything goes. *What did she tell her?* I thought.

"Yes?"

"She told me the good news."

"Oh, about Bryce?"

"I never knew he had it in him."

"Neither did I. I suppose he's a secret romantic," I said.

"You must have done some convincing!"

"I didn't talk to her," I blurted out.

She looked up at me, eyebrows raised in confusion. "You didn't?"

"No. I took your advice. Bryce is a grown man, he needed to solve his own problems. Probably wouldn't have done anyone any good if I talked to her."

"Well, it all worked out at the end, didn't it?" Alison said.

"Sure."

We stood in front of the coffee shop and kissed again before we went in. She ordered two caramel frappuccinos and a large black coffee.

"You want anything?" she asked.

"I'm good," I replied.

We dropped off the coffee back at her dorm and finished watching *The Notebook* with the girls. I fell asleep before they both died at the end. I woke up to the girls sobbing.

"Don't worry, their love will live on," I joked.

"Shut up, Cooper. You don't even know," Joanna said with tears streaming down her chubby face. "Asshole."

"I feel a lot of love in this room."

Alison wiped away a tear and shut off the TV. "Well, I think it's past Joanna's bedtime."

"I should get back," Dawn said.

"We'll walk with you" Alison said, wrapping her arm around me.

"Back to Cabot?" I said.

"Yeah, I mean we shouldn't let Dawn go by herself this late at night. Besides, you can protect me from any banditos," she grinned with her chin pressed against my chest.

"Really, I'll be fine." Dawn protested

"Don't be silly."

I had no choice but to go. Cabot Hall was only a ten-minute walk, but it felt like an eternity. Alison and Dawn discussed the literary quality of *Fifty Shades of Grey,* which Alison considered being nothing more but intriguing mommy porn. Dawn thoroughly enjoyed it.

"You're quiet," Alison said to me.

Adrenaline rushed through me as though I were up on the mound with a runner on. We approached the red doors beneath the etched slab of Cabot Hall. I remembered I was wearing the same windbreaker. I quickly took it off.

"You okay?" Alison asked.

"Oh, sorry. Just hot," I said.

We entered Cabot. There was no one by the stairs. They seemed to stretch to eternity. We arrived at Dawn's floor, and I felt like a spy on a secret mission, hoping not to get caught. As we approached Dawn's room, I felt relieved.

"Hey!"

A cheery voice shot from behind us. I turned to find the girl I'd seen the other night, the one who'd been wearing the wet towel. "Brought some friends, I see," she said to Dawn.

"They were just walking me back from Alison's dorm, Kristen." Kristen twisted her head in curiosity as she examined me from down the hall.

"I've seen you before." Kristen said.

"He's a starting pitcher for the Silverbacks. He's famous," Alison said, before giving me a raspberry.

"No, that's not it," Kristen said, as she approached me with caution. Silence pierced through my nerves. "Oh my God!" Kristen shrieked.

Blood rushed from my face.

"Has anyone said you look like Jimmy from Shameless?"

Alison jumped in glee with agreement. "Oh my God, he does, doesn't he?!"

Dawn didn't seem to care.

"Hey, did you ever call campus police?" Kristen said after a moment.

"Campus police?"

Dawn fidgeted, but kept her cool.

"Police? What for?" Alison asked, concerned.

"It was nothing. Someone jerk looking through my door while I was studying. He ran off before I got to the door. Kristen was the one who saw him."

"It didn't sound like you were studying," she joked.

Dawn cringed.

"You had the TV on so loud I could hear it down the hall. Anyway, couldn't see him well in the dark. Raquel was downstairs studying when she saw him run out the door. Nobody got a good look at his face."

"I never called the police. Didn't see the point. Besides, it was probably some fraternity prank. You know how those idiots are," Dawn added. More lies and secrets. Dawn's were beautiful, smooth. They just rolled off of her tongue, one after another.

"You can't be too careful these days," I said.

"He sort of had your build, though," Kristen said.

"Really?"

"What can you do? I would keep the door closed from now on though," Kristen advised.

"Thanks, Mom. You want to join us for some wine?"

"No thanks. I have a Spanish exam I have to cram for tonight. See ya," She said before returning to her dorm.

Dawn's room was cramped for three people, but it was clean and well kept. She closed the door. Dawn opened the window, letting in the cool Gulf air. She popped open the bottle of Merlot from Chatwick Liquors and Bar, a favorite Tampa State watering hole.

She took out some plastic cups from one of her cabinet drawers. "Sorry. Couldn't afford wine glasses. Next best thing, I guess."

I offered to pour the wine. "What should we toast to?" Dawn asked.

"World peace?" I joked.

"Something that doesn't conflict with the nature of humanity, Coop," Alison said.

"Okay, fine then. To the little things." Our cups kissed.

"Good, isn't it?" Dawn said.

"Not bad," I murmured. I wouldn't say I had much of a palate for it.

Dawn's cell phone rang. She checked it and put in on vibrate and lay it on her night table. The phone gyrated on the table as it buzzed from the incoming call. It kept buzzing, the caller on the other line making repeated attempts. She checked the phone again.

"Aren't you going to get that?" I asked. I had my suspicions who was on the other line. Dawn closed the door behind her as she entered the hallway.

"I can't talk now...." I heard the low drone of her voice from inside her dorm.

Alison leaned her head against my chest as we sat on the floor and drank wine. Dawn came back with a worried expression on her face.

"Everything okay?" asked Alison. "Is Bryce…?"

"I'm sorry to be so curt, but I think you guys should go," Dawn said, her eyebrows pinching together..

"We just got here. Can we at least finish the wine?" Alison scoffed.

"Sorry."

"That wouldn't have been Bryce wanting a little late night rendezvous, would it?" asked Alison.

"No. Just a classmate asking a question about the Chem exam tomorrow."

Alison and I left Cabot, but my mind swirled with suspicion. Dawn and Buckhorn. I left Alison at her dorm and went for a stroll around campus, wandering toward Brass Field. It was dark. The mosquitos swarmed around the one floodlight lit by the storage shed.

The field looked like a museum, with the brown rust of the bleachers reminding me it would still be here long after I was rotting beneath the earth. I felt fear that night. Real fear. I had not been able to identify it for sometime, but now it was here and it was impossible to escape.

The more time I spent away from Alison, the more I fell in love with her. I became conflicted between love and hate. Love for Alison. Hate for anything that left a void or made me feel inferior in. Alison was the light at the end of tunnel. She gave me a sense peace that somehow, things were going to be OK.

I still loved baseball, but the stress of competition and the pressure to win was getting the best of me. Baseball didn't seem fun anymore. It wasn't the children's game I remembered.

The turmoil had been eating me up inside. I wasn't sure who I was becoming. I had begun losing control and I knew it. My heart raced. I paced outside the field, thinking about what I'd done and what I was capable of doing. The battle for my soul waged inside of me as my secret fears were getting the best of me.

# Chapter 17

Brass Field looked heavenly as the morning sun rose on the horizon, ushering in a new day of practice. I was warming up when Buckhorn trotted onto the field, uniform and all.

"Look at this guy," Samson said. "Who the hell does he think he is?"

"Apparently the coach," Zach said.

"He's just advising. That's all," Bryce said.

"Buckhorn's not a ball player," Zach said. "Not baseball, anyway."

We started with calisthenics. Pushups, suicide sit-ups, long runs. Buckhorn ran practice like a boot camp. "Hey, Coach, what is this? My feet hurt," Samson joked. Dawson wasn't amused. Neither were the rest of us.

Finally, we got to play some actual baseball. I pitched in the bullpen, methodically working on my mechanics. Buckhorn stood only a few feet away, observing me from behind those Ray Bans with his hands behind his back.

He sickened me in more ways than one. I hated him. It was different from how I felt about Bryce. There was no confusion or empathy with Buckhorn. It was pure hatred. He didn't seem human. Then again, I feared I was no longer human myself. I was flesh and bone, but my mind was transforming, entering a realm I never thought existed. A realm most of us feared to go. But it seemed I was no longer afraid of that. I was at home there. And that's what scared me the most.

Buckhorn gathered us after practice. There was a fundraising gala at the end of the week in the old banquet ballroom on campus. Buckhorn wanted the school's prized athletic possessions there on display for all the pageantry. We all had to wear suits. Buckhorn offered to pay for the suit rentals, considering formal wear wasn't the usual attire that hung in our dorm room closets. And we were allowed to bring a date.

"Oh, I get to dress up!" Alison exclaimed when I told her. "You'll get to look all dapper! How exciting! What's the event for?"

"It's a fundraising event. Buckhorn just wants to show us off."

"You don't seem too excited about it."

"I'm not one for pomp and circumstance," I said.

Alison fixed the collar of my shirt. "I think it's going to be a big night for you. I'm proud of you."

I turned my head, grinned and grabbed her hand. "Really?"

"Maybe you don't realise this, but you've accomplished a lot more than you think. You're smart, determined. You got a lot going for you. I wish I was as focused as you. Sometimes I wake up and get anxious at the thought of not knowing where my life is headed. But when I'm with you, it gives me hope that things will turn out alright."

I ran my hand through her hair and held her. She looked up at me and planted her chin on my chest. "Aren't you going to say anything?" Alison said.

I kissed her on the forehead and whispered in her ear. "Actions speak louder than words."

Bryce and I escorted Dawn and Alison to the mall so that they could pick out their dresses. We stopped by the food court to get some pizza while the girls shopped.

I've never seen someone eat a slice of pizza so fast in my entire life. I don't think Bryce even chewed. The girls eventually joined us, drinking smoothies from the juice bar. We strolled around the mall.

There was a mini golf course called Palmer's Arcade located at the end of the mall. "Who's up for mini golf?" Alison said enthusiastically. I cringed. The last time I played mini golf was at my thirteenth birthday party and I vomited because I had too much pizza and ice cream.

Inside there were several rows of old arcade machines, reminiscent of another era. Kids ran from one arcade machine to another, part of a birthday party held in the party room adjacent to the indoor golf course. Alison's white shirt glowed from the neon lighting.

Bryce stood behind Dawn and gripped her hands, demonstrating a proper swing He snuck a kiss on her cheek before she tapped the ball with her club. Dawn was a horrendous mini golf player, though I wasn't much better. Alison was the pro among us, precise in both her swing and predicting the ball's trajectory.

She hit a hole in one on the 9th hole.

"Tiger Woods of mini golf over here," I called out.

She stuck her tongue out and pecked me on the cheek. A surge of warmth ran through me. I liked it. We breezed through each hole, handily beating Bryce and Dawn by five strokes. Alison waved the scorecard in Bryce and Dawn's faces.

"Next time, Alison, next time," Bryce said.

"Can't be good at everything, I guess," I said to Bryce, giving him a playful shove.

"Guess not," he replied.

"Oh, Dawn and I need to do a little more shopping. Do you boys mind?"

I sighed. "How much longer do you need? We've been here for three hours!" I said.

"Lord, you've never shopped with a woman, have you?" Alison

said. I rolled my eyes. "We won't be long, hun. Besides you want us to look good for you, right?" she said slyly.

Bryce and I killed time with some arcade games while the girls shopped. I lost at Pac Man. Bryce preferred racing games, spilling all his quarters into the machines. For a moment, we pretended to be children, where the world was a different place.

I briefly forgot about secrets, about empathy, about rage. It was a reprieve from my own conflict with lunacy. When we ran out of quarters Bryce and I left Palmer's arcade in search of Dawn and Alison, leaving my adolescence behind.

The day of the fundraising event had arrived. I was in the bathroom getting ready. I wiped the condensation from the bathroom mirror. I combed my hair back, and applied gel to make it firm and stylish. I stared into the mirror, analyzing every single wrinkle, pimple, and flaw on my face. I took a dab of face cream and rubbed it in, hoping it would hide most of the wrinkles. I put on more cream when I noticed a strand of gray hair sticking out from the side of me head. I yanked it out and held in in my hand. "Fuck," I said.

I turned my head, looking back at my reflection with curiosity. I took deep breaths, taking in the flaws that I had a harder time disguising.

I heard a knock. "What do you think?" Bryce said, showing up in his suit.

"Oh, you're so handsome," Zach said, smacking Bryce in the ass with an open palm.

"Hey, watch it, jerk, this is a rental!" Bryce said. "So, what do you think? Lady killer, huh?"

"Lookin' good, friend," I said.

"I can get used to this. Suit and all. Makes me feel important."

"You *should* get used to it. You have to look good when you make it to the pros. You can't wear that crap you usually wear here," I said.

"Jeans, flip flops, and a 'Kiss me I'm Irish' shirt aren't crap, Coop. That's fine collegiate apparel." Bryce wasn't even Irish, but he figured that shirt was a good conversation starter with the ladies. I used to rag on him about it all the time. The shirt could have walked on its own. That's how many times he wore it. He had retired it junior year, but he still caved into the urge to wear it from time to time.

I changed into my black suit and adjusted my tie in the bathroom mirror, still moist with condensation from my recent shower.

The gala was to begin at seven. Bryce and I went our separate ways to pick up our dates for the evening. I knocked on Alison's door.

"Just a minute," Alison called. A minute slowly grew to five.

"Come on, it's getting late," I said, pacing up and down the hall.

"Almost done," she said.

The door swung open. She was breathtaking. She wore a dark blue, skin-tight dress, her leg was seductively exposed by a long slit in her dress. Her makeup extenuated her natural beauty. I stood amazed at how beautiful she looked.

I stammered a bit before I could say something coherent. "You're beautiful," I said stroking her hair.

"You think so? Joanna did the make-up." She said while she fiddled with her dress and patted her hair.

"Absolutely!" I said.

"Shush," Alison said. "Come in while I finish up."

"We really should be going," I said.

"Have you ever heard of being fashionably late? Relax, I'll just be another moment."

I reclined in Alison's desk chair as she rushed to the bathroom to finish up. Joanna lay on her bed, reading her American History textbook as I waited. An aura of awkwardness floated between us.

"You did a good job on the make-up," I said, yawning and stretching my arms.

Joanna glanced at me before returning to her page. "Thanks. Who are you two trying to impress?"

"It's a fundraising event."

"Ah," Joanna said in an enlightened moment. "Raising money for what?"

"What do you care?" I asked.

Joanna glared at me. "What does that girl see in you?"

It was only a few minutes' walk to the banquet hall. The main academic and administrative building on campus was topped with Moorish minarets, domes and cupolas. Originally built in the late 1800s as a hotel, it had been converted into the university in the 1940's, the campus expanding around the building in the years since. Though renovated, its Victorian style still shone through.

The banquet hall was down a long hallway lined with several classrooms and offices. We followed the sea of attendees approaching the main entrance of the hall.

"Big turnout," Alison said.

Zach walked toward us with a grinning Kayla on his arm. I found myself sweating as I took in the black cocktail dress she wore, hoping Alison wouldn't notice the beads of sweat dripping from my forehead. She smirked at me when she saw Alison and me near the hors d'oeuvres.

"Looking good," Zach said to us.

"Thanks."

"Hi, I'm Kayla," Kayla said, extending her hand out to me.

"Pleasure to meet you," I said, shaking her hand with a forced smile. "This is Alison," I added, not wanting to forget.

"HI! Wow, you look amazing. I love that dress," Kayla said to Alison.

"Really? I wish I could fit into a dress like yours. My ass jiggles when I have a cupcake," Alison said.

Kayla and Alison excused themselves, heading to the girls' room to gossip. I wondered what Kayla would tell her.

I turned to Zach and pinched his arm. "You didn't tell me she was your date!"

"Sorry. Sort of last minute," Zach said.

"Not cool, man."

"Oh relax. Besides, you guys didn't do anything. Completely innocent. Except for the raging hard on you probably had." Zach noticed my concern. "Don't worry, she won't say anything. She's not stupid."

"You're something else, Zach," I said shaking my head.

"Where's Bryce?" Zach said looking around.

I shrugged. "He should be here. We both left at the same time."

"Damn hornball. He and Dawn must be fornicating as we speak."

Samson arrived with a turquoise suit, without a date, to no one's surprise.

"What's up, losers?"

"Samson, this is a black tie event, hence the color black."

Samson bobbed his head, out of sync to the classical music that was playing in the background. "I want to stand out. I just read this book called *The Game*. It's called the peacock theory. I have to stand out to attract a mate. Preferably one with very large breasts," He said gawking at a brunette who strolled past him.

"You are a strange little man, Samson," I said.

Samson gave me a double thumbs up. "Peacock theory, Coop. Peacock theory."

Alison and Kayla returned and laughed at Samson. "Um, what in the world are you wearing?" Kayla asked.

"What the hell do you think I'm wearing?"

"Not sure, to be quite honest," Alison said.

"He's trying to attract a mate," Zach said.

"Good luck with that," Kayla said, joining in the chorus of laughter.

"Samson," Coach Dawson yelled. The two went outside the banquet hall for a chat, presumably in relation to Samson's exotic attire.

Bryce and Dawn strolled in. Bryce slapping hands with some members of the team.

"You see, we're not the only ones fashionably late," Alison commented.

"Look at all of these stiffs," said Bryce, measuring the crowd of rich donors, students, and professors, all of them sticking in their respective little groups.

"These stiffs are why we're here, Bryce old boy. To impress them. That's where that charm of yours will be the most useful," Zach said.

"I suppose you're right," Bryce replied. Then he saw Kayla. "Hey, I know you, aren't you—?"

"Say, why don't we all get something to drink?" Zach interrupted, grabbing Bryce by the arm. "I'm parched."

"Great idea," I said.

I waited in line, rummaging through my pockets hoping to find some singles.

"It's an open bar," Kayla said. She was standing behind me. I ordered Alison a rum and coke while I got a beer. Kayla ordered a White Russian.

"I like my drinks sweet," she said as she put her lips on the glass, staining it with her red lipstick. "Don't worry. I didn't say anything. Alison seems like a great girl. I can see why you didn't make a pass at me," she said, looking over to Alison talking with Bryce and Zach at their table.

"She is," I said. "Are you and Zach...?"

"Oh no. I was just doing him a favor. He needed a date and I was available. Besides, a girl can't refuse an excuse to dress up nice while getting free drinks."

"Understandable."

"You look good, by the way," Kayla sipped, licking some of the drink that had spilled onto her finger.

"So do you."

"Don't let Alison catch you saying that," Kayla said with a raised eyebrow.

I laughed. "She would probably agree with me."

"So, what's this all about?" Kayla said pointing her chin at the crowd.

"Kissing the butts of wealthy donors."

"Interesting," Kayla said. "You don't seem like the ass-kissing type."

I scoffed. "What makes you say that?"

"A hunch."

"Trying to steal my date, are we?" Zach said, arriving with a dry martini in his hand. "Who wants the olive?"

"I do," Kayla said. She ate the olive from its cocktail stick. "Yummy."

"Who should we pucker up to first?" Zach asked me.

"I don't know who any of these people are," I replied.

"They're rich, that's all we need to know. My kind of people."

"You're rich?" I asked Zach.

"Wealth is not just measured in money, though it would be very nice to have a few extra zeros in my checking account. I consider myself rich with other luxuries. Friendship, sex, baseball, sex, good wine, sex. Did I mention sex?"

"You're too much," Kayla said, not taking her eyes off of me as she finished off her White Russian.

I realized that I'd lost sight of Alison. I searched through the sea of guests until I found her by the podium on the stage. She was laughing, playing with her hair as Buckhorn spoke to her with all his charm and grace.

Bryce and Dawn stood only a few feet away, speaking with some guest. Dawn looked over her shoulder, glaring at Alison.

"Excuse me." I rushed through the swarm of guests, growing agitated by their inability to see I was trying to get by, until I finally reached Alison and Buckhorn.

"Hey Coop, we were just talking about you," Alison said, kissing me on the cheek.

"No wonder I felt my ears burning," I said with a stilted laugh.

Buckhorn was just as phony, but he was good at concealing it. His smile, his charm, it was all a disguise to hide something more cunning. But who was I to talk?

Buckhorn shook hands with a few guests before he patted me on the shoulder. "Alison was telling me she's planning on going to grad school," Buckhorn said.

Alison went on and on about writing and potential MFA programs. Buckhorn's eyes glanced around the room, smiling and waving at guests while Alison spoke.

"There you are." Bryce and Dawn arrived with drinks in hand. Dawn avoided looking at Buckhorn. Their connection was so obvious to me, but the others were oblivious.

"Dawn, did you tell everyone the good news?" Buckhorn asked. Dawn looked up in surprise at Buckhorn's announcement. "You didn't tell them?"

Dawn said, fidgeting with her drink. "I got into grad school at the University of Texas,"

"That's great, Dawn!" Alison said.

"That's news to me." Bryce frowned, biting his lip.

"I have a few contacts at UT. They just bumped up her application. But her grades did all the work. The science department will be lucky to have you," Buckhorn said.

Dawn put her drink on the stage behind us. "Excuse me, I need to use the restroom," she said before rushing off. Bryce started to follow her when Buckhorn grabbed him by the arm.

"Why don't we meet some of our distinguished guests, Bryce?"

Many of the guests were prominent figures in the Tampa business community, as well as some of Buckhorn's buddies from investment banking. He showed us off like prized possessions, boasting about the Silverbacks' performance so far that year. Some of the donors were impressed, others were indifferent, others didn't care in the slightest.

Steve Herman, the owner of one of the largest IT accounting firms in the southeast, nearly spilled his drink on my suit as he barged between us to greet his former colleague. Buckhorn gave him a bear hug, lifting him off the ground with relative ease. The two of them carried on like boisterous and obnoxious frat boys who never grew up.

Alison joined Zach and Kayla by the bar. Bryce searched for Dawn, who still hadn't returned from the bathroom. Meanwhile, I had Steve Herman's brash voice in my ear.

"So Patrick, I want you two to be honest with me. How much fur do you get? Come on, you can tell me!" Steve laughed obnoxiously, a sound like he was gasping for air but was really just doing his very best to act like a jerk.

"Easy there, Steve," Buckhorn said with a clenched smile.

"Alright, alright, sorry. So let me ask you another question, why the hell should I give one red cent to this sorry excuse of a school?" Steve asked, laughing. "No offense, Patrick."

Patrick went through his usual sales pitch. Bragging about the Business School's high ranking in US and World Report. The research grants earned by the science departments. And, of course, Silverback athletics.

"Damn, you were signed by the Pirates. Nice," Steve said.

"Sure," said Bryce, still distracted looking for Dawn.

"You're going to get so much tail." Steve's head might as well been on a swivel as he gawked at almost every attractive women he could get his eyes on. How he'd managed to become the owner and president of a major company was beyond me, but Buckhorn, being the smooth talker he was, convinced Steve to give a donation of five thousand dollars in between the repulsive, sexist drivel.

"Don't spend it all in one place," Steve joked.

"Excuse me, I'll be back," Bryce said, noticing Dawn at the back of the hall.

"Don't be long. We got a lot of people to meet," Buckhorn told him.

Bryce nodded and made his way to Dawn. Buckhorn and I were left alone. I sipped my drink and admired the throngs of people that continued to enter the hall. A crowd of people surrounded a red haired women moving through the groups of guests who waited to greet Janet Marquis, as fashionably late as anyone could be without being insulting about it.

"Patrick." Janet motioned for us to meet her by a group of donors. One of them, Dr. Menendez, owned a prominent spinal surgery practice. They were joined by his wife, the owner of a boutique clothing store in Tampa and author of several self-published children's books. Coach Dawson joined us when Janet wagged his finger at him from his spot at the bar. Coach Dawson extended to shake his hand at Janet who only nodded and introduced us like we were an afterthought.

"I hear the team is doing great this year," Dr. Menendez said. "I played from 72-73, right fielder. Sure miss those days. Of course we weren't as good as the team you have now. What are you doing differently this year, Coach?"

Coach was about to answer when Buckhorn interrupted. "It's a combination of personnel and training, and a little bit of luck doesn't hurt either. And having a pitcher like Coop sure helps."

"I hear you're one hell of a player," Dr. Mendez said. "You think you can help bring us home a championship this year?"

"I hope so. Anything to get this slave driver off our backs," I said, playfully hitting Buckhorn's arm with my elbow. A pretentious and awkward laugh erupted. Buckhorn managed a forced grin.

"What position do you play again?" Dr. Menendez's wife asked.

"Pitcher."

"Really? Are you any good? I heard one your players was signed by a professional team."

I wanted to throw my drink on her.

Dawson said, "He's seven and two this season. He's one of the reasons we made it this far."

"But there is always room for improvement," Buckhorn added.

"I'll be the judge of that," Dawson responded. "Why don't you tell us how many years you played baseball, Patrick?"

The donor's' eyes glittered with curiosity. "I played football for Notre Dame," Patrick said with a wide and proud smile, toasting to his alma mater with his martini. The donors were impressed. Dawson wasn't.

"So I suppose that doesn't make you a good judge of talent as far as baseball's concerned, does it, Patrick?"

"Athletes are one and the same, Coach. Of all people, you should know that. You're the coach, last time I checked," Buckhorn mumbled underneath his breath.

"That's right. I am the coach. And it seems like you've never coached anything a day in your life."

Janet quickly changed the subject, talking on and on about the school and its academic credentials. But the conversation always seemed to return to baseball, making her nostrils flare in annoyance. If it were up to her, she would have scrapped the entire athletic program. But she needed us just as much as we needed her, so she played nice like the politician she was.

"What the hell was that all about?" Janet asked Dawson once the donors moved on.

"Just making a point," Dawson said.

"You were out of line, Coach," Buckhorn said pointing his finger at Coach.

"Is that right?"

"Enough! Both of you!" Janet hissed. "You are here to help raise money for this school, not bicker like a bunch of overgrown jocks. Now I expect you two to cut out this nonsense and fraternize with our guests. Understood?"

"Of course," Buckhorn replied.

"Jocks," Janet muttered, shaking her head as she went to mingle.

"You trying to embarrass me?" Buckhorn snapped, jabbing his finger in Dawson's chest. He shoved it away before I got in between the two of them.

"I think we can all use a drink, huh? Right, Coach?"

"No. I think I'm done here. I'll see you on the field, Coop," Coach said.

"I'll be there, Coach."

Buckhorn drank his martini while he eyed Dawson leaving the hall. "Man doesn't hold back. You gotta admire the guy," he said.

"I do," I said, looking for someone I knew so I get away from him.

"Alison, she's a great girl," Buckhorn said.

"I know."

"How much are you emotionally invested in her?"

I cocked my head and took a deep breath. "I never looked at her as in investment. I think you spent too much time in banking."

Buckhorn nodded with a grin and took a tip from his drink. "Everything is an investment. Money, energy, emotions; they're all commodities we trade for time, Coop. It's all about prioritizing. What's most important to you?"

"Alison doesn't concern you," I said.

Buckhorn moved closer. "And sneaking around, peeking into other people's dorms in the middle of the night concerns you?"

My chin quivered. He got so close I could smell his aftershave that made my eyes water.

"I'm a very observant man, Coop. I think you figured that out by now. Nothing gets past me." He smiled, a sickening amusement filling his eyes. "Did you enjoy watching us?"

I couldn't say anything. My mind raced with different thoughts that amounted to absolutely nothing. I looked around the room for Bryce and Dawn. They were nowhere to found.

"Why?"

For a moment Buckhorn didn't said nothing. He finally just shrugged his shoulders and nodded with a wink.

"I'm sure the NCAA would love to hear about this."

"Oh right, well, perhaps. But Dawn is not going to ruin her chances of getting into grad school. You don't have a shred of proof. No one saw us except you. Besides, you were trespassing in a non-co-ed dorm, spying on a female student. Wouldn't look good on your part."

"I'll take my chances. And what about Bryce? You know how he feels about her," I said.

"I do. But that will soon pass. He'll be moving on into bigger and better things."

"Why do this?" I asked.

"Because I can," Buckhorn said before Janet emerged from behind me.

"Patrick. You're set to speak in a few minutes," she said.

"Sure, Janet. Enjoy the rest of the event, Coop," Patrick said.

Everyone took their seats. I sat with Zach, Kayla, and Alison.

"Where's Bryce and Dawn?" Alison asked.

"Who knows? When are they serving the food? I'm starving," Zach said.

I stood up.

"Where are you going?" Alison asked.

"I'll be right back."

I went outside the banquet hall and searched for Bryce down the long stretch of hallway. I found Bryce and Dawn arguing. She pulled herself away from him and ran off. I watched Bryce return with his head down, looking defeated.

"I was looking for you," I said. "Everything okay?"

"I need a drink," he said. I followed him back into the hall. He walked straight to the bar and I returned to the table. Bryce sat beside Alison.

"Hey, where's Dawn?" Alison asked.

"She had to leave," Bryce said, drinking his beer.

"Why?"

"Wasn't feeling well."

We fell silent as we listened to Buckhorn's speech. Zach leaned over and whispered in my ear. "It's tonight."

"Tonight?"

"Over in the gymnasium at midnight."

"I don't think this is a good time," I said, motioning to Bryce as he sulked in his chair.

"It has to be tonight. It's important, Coop. We have to resolve this. This being a championship run and all."

"You have impeccable timing," I said.

"Look. It won't take long. It's an informal hearing. That's all. It's more symbolic than anything else. We owe it to Bryce and the team."

"Bryce is in no condition for this 'informal meeting' or whatever the hell you want to call it."

"What are you two mumbling about over there?" Kayla asked.

"Yeah, maybe you two should be each other's dates," Alison said, giggling until she noticed Bryce's scowl. "Rough crowd."

Several other speakers took their turns as dinner was served. Bryce barely ate his food.

"Not hungry?"

Bryce stared down at his food and cut into the steak, only taking one bite. "I'm not that hungry." Bryce said before leaving the table. I stood to follow him when Alison grabbed my arm.

"What's wrong?" Alison asked. "Is Bryce okay?"

"I'll call you later, OK?" I said.

Zach reminded me of the hearing with a subtle glance and a raised eyebrow.

I followed Bryce outside. The sky was dark as a storm made its way over Tampa Bay. Thunder reverberated in the distance. "Bryce, what happened with Dawn?"

"I don't get her, Coop," he said.

Bryce watched the rain fall, the rain drops thick and heavy. The wind rushed through the campus grounds, causing the trees to sway and scatter twigs and leaves all over the wet ground.

"Bryce, there's something I need to talk to you about," I said.

"Not now, Coop," Bryce said.

"It's about Dawn."

"What about her?"

Time ceased to exist. Bryce, broken and pitiful. A man once filled with vigor had become nothing more than a pile of emotional garbage unable to pull himself out of his funk. I wanted to tell him. I really did. I yearned to see him suffer. To see him self-destruct from his own emotions. I took pride that I could do that at a moment's notice. But my empathy kept rearing its head.

I tried to tell him, but couldn't, only reminding him that Dawn was a great girl and he should be patient with her. He walked away into the rain. I told him to come back, but he marched on, not caring the slightest bit for the torrential downpour that fell upon him.

# Chapter 18

It was late in the evening. I waited in our dorm, but there was no sign of Bryce. The gala ended at ten, but I left shortly after Bryce. I told Alison I would call her, but I was afraid to pick up the phone. I was tired of keeping secrets. I felt nauseous from the under cooked steak, but the rain that beat on my window eased my tension.

In an hour I was to head to the gymnasium. I dozed off when I heard a knock on the door. "Who is it?"

Zach entered the room. I saw Kayla lingering in the hallway.

"Where's Bryce?" he asked.

"I don't know."

"You were the last one to see him."

"He didn't tell me where he was going. I think he got into another argument with Dawn."

"Over what?"

"Not sure. Maybe you should ask him that."

"I would if I could find him, but he's not answering his phone. Tonight's important. He has to be there or it won't work. Find him."

I got up and opened the blinds. "It's raining outside."

"I'm sure he's not far. Probably going for a run for all we know."

"I can go with you," Kayla said. "Wouldn't want you alone in the rain."

I asked Zach why he didn't go, but said he needed to head to the gymnasium to make sure all the chairs were set up and everyone was accounted for. I took a black umbrella from my closet. The rain still came down hard, but the lightning subsided at least. Kayla huddled with me underneath the umbrella. She wrapped her arms around one of mine. Her perfume was enticing and sweet. "Where do you think he is?" She asked.

"Not sure. He couldn't have gone far. He might be in the weight room or going for a run."

"Even in the rain?"

"He does sometimes."

"Why don't you try Dawn's dorm?" she asked.

I wanted to avoid it, but I knew of all the places available to him, he had to be there. We walked past Alison's dorm. Her light was on. A girl with a purple umbrella ran past us through the rain towards Alison's dorm, jumping over a puddle of water before reaching the main entrance. Her pink rain boots flashed as she swept inside.

The brick facade of Cabot Hall soon became visible. The door to Dawn's dorm room was closed. We knocked. No answer.

"Maybe she's with Bryce," Kayla said.

The rain subsided. We went back outside. Kayla grabbed my arm again, this time holding my hand. The night cool from the rain.

"I'm cold," Kayla said. I offered her my rain jacket, but she wrapped her arms around me instead. I could've kissed her. To show Alison she wasn't the only one with secrets. But I didn't.

As we made our way back, I noticed a figure wandering outside the athletic building. At first I thought it was Miguel, but as he came closer, I recognized the slump of those broad shoulders.. "Bryce!" I yelled.

He kept walking as if he hadn't heard me. Kayla and I approached him. His eyes were red, gazing off into the distance.

"You okay? We've been looking all over for you," Kayla said.

"I uh, just wanted to go for a walk," Bryce said, looking back at the athletic department.

"In the rain, silly?" Kayla said.

"Where's Dawn?" I asked.

He took off his suit jacket and slung it over his shoulder. "I think I'm going back to the dorm."

"I'll come with you."

Zach found us in the rain, and herded our reluctant group towards the gymnasium. I wanted to get the trial over with. I viewed it as another chance to hurt Bryce, to watch him suffer as he wondered what my intentions were. I would play with his mind while the team watched, thinking my intentions were pure.

The main entrance was locked, so we entered through the first floor fire escape door held open with a rock. It was dark down the corridor leading to the home team locker room.

"I can barely see a thing," Kayla said.

"We're almost there. Just past the corner," I said.

We turned a corner and into the main hall. At the other end were the Silverbacks baseball team, seated on rows of folding chairs. They turned towards us once they heard the squeak of our shoes against the gymnasium floor.

"What is all this?" Bryce said.

"You'll see."

Zach directed us to several chairs that faced the rows of players. Samson sat in the front row. His obnoxious grin grew the moment Bryce and I sat.

"Kayla, you don't have to be here," Zach said. "I'm curious," she said as she took an empty seat in the third row.

Zach positioned himself front and center on our would-be stage, acting as judge, and perhaps juror and executioner.

"So Coop, tell me, how long have you been playing for Tampa State?" he asked.

"I think everyone here knows the answer to that," I replied.

"It's just for the sake of starting things off. So, tell us, how long have you been playing?"

"Four years now."

Bryce stood from his chair. "What the hell is all this about, Zach? We're sitting in a steaming hot gymnasium like a bunch of assholes, asking ourselves stupid questions like as if this was some sort of fucking trial."

"We're doing this for the team, Bryce. If you can just be patient you'll understand what it is I'm trying to do," Zach said walking closer to Bryce.

"How do you know what it is I need! I don't have time for this. This whole thing is stupid!" Bryce said standing up from his chair when some of the guys grabbed him by the shoulders, encouraging him to stay. He paced around a bit before he settled down back in his chair. Bryce nodded in appreciation and re-asked the question.

"Let me ask you again, Coop. How long have you been friends with, Bryce?"

I sighed. "I said four years."

Zach nodded in agreement. He began asking questions, most notably about how things were at home as well as my love life, which I was embarrassed to discuss considering that Kayla was in attendance and I thought it was nobody's business. Zach kept it kosher and moved on to questions regarding my academic standing, which was better than the entire Silverbacks team put together.

"Were you surprised coach made you co-captain?"

A drone of conversation erupted from the audience. Zach shushed them quiet. "Were you?"

I sighed. "I suppose."

"Do you think you've earned the right to be captain?"

I glared at Zach, crossing my arms trying to hold back saying something I would regret. "Yes I do."

Zach pulled out a piece of paper and read my stats. Even I didn't realize how good I was. I wasn't sure what he was driving at. It wasn't to compliment my ego or impress the team by any stretch of the imagination. "And here is the most notable stat of all," Zach said. "You haven't hit one batter since freshman year. Until Bryce."

Samson groaned in his chair. "Just ask already, Zach! I don't have all night."

Zach turned and looked directly at me.

"Did you hit Bryce on purpose?"

Bryce awoke from his depressed state, surprise clouding his face. "What kind of question is that?" he asked.

"It's a fair question, Bryce," Zach said.

My voice quivered. But I wanted to laugh. "Of course I didn't," I said. "Why would I do such a thing? That's a damn stupid question, Zach."

"You haven't hit one batter in thirty five career starts."

"It was an accident. The ball was slippery."

"Did wanting to throw ninety have something to do with it?"

"What?"

"You were pretty keen on reaching that magic number. Perhaps your competitiveness got the best of you? You had to let your frustrations out on somebody?"

I stared him down. "So why Bryce?"

"Because, he's your catcher. Maybe you blame him for not hitting ninety."

"That's bullshit!"

"You haven't been signed by anybody, correct?"

"What does that have to with it?"

"That's enough!" Bryce jumped from his chair and stood face to face with Zach. "It wasn't intentional."

"Let's ask some of the others what they think," Zach said.

One by one, each player was interrogated by Zach. Most of the guys went through the motions. They were indifferent at best. Most of them thought I was innocent. When it was his turn, Samson swaggered up to the front. I adjusted my chair as my throwing hand began to tremble. Samson, with his arms crossed, grinned with such delight as Zach began to question him.

"Do you think Cooper hit Bryce on purpose?" Zach said.

"Maybe."

"What do you mean, maybe?" Zach asked.

"I don't know. Who knows what's going on in that brain of his."

"What makes you think he did it intentionally?"

"Because Coop is not who you think he is," Samson said.

"Go on," Zach pressed.

"Coop is one of those guys who has to pretend to be something he's not. In other words—" Samson rushed towards me and shoved his finger in my face. "—he's a phony."

He broke out in laughter and turned to face the audience with his arms out. "But hell, we're all phonies, right?"

Zach rolled his eyes. "Thanks, Samson. Have a seat."

"Are we done here?" I asked.

"Not quite." Zach placed his hand on Bryce's shoulder.

"I'm not up for this, man," Bryce said, wiping the perspiration from his eyes.

"It's for your own good. We're doing this for you."

"If you are then you'll understand why I don't want to take part in this," Bryce replied.

"Why. Is something wrong?"

Bryce's leg twitched. He let out a loud sigh and cracked his knuckles. "It's nothing," he said.

"Nothing? It's obviously something," Zach said.

"It doesn't concern you. Any of you."

Zach pressed his hand on Bryce's shoulder and patted him on the back. "Just a few questions."

Bryce nodded.

"How long have you caught for Coop, Bryce?" Zach asked.

"Four years."

"So you know Coop's mannerisms. Strength and weaknesses. How he thinks, up on the mound?"

"Sure."

Zach rubbed his chin and paced around Bryce. "So, did you find it odd that Coop hit you that day with a fastball?"

"I never gave it much thought, considering I don't remember much of it."

"You never gave it much thought?" Zach pressed

"Yeah. I mean accidents happen."

"Sure they do. But you heard Coop's stats. He's never hit a batter before you."

"There's a first time for everything."

"Have you two always gotten along?"

"Sure."

"Never any disagreements?"

Bryce threw his hands in disgust. "Look. I know Coop. He's a good kid. He would never try to hurt me intentionally. What happened that day was an accident. Pure and simple. I know you're looking out for the team and all, but I wouldn't want anyone else on the mound but him. He's my friend. I don't know what the hell this damn meeting is all about but it's a bunch of bullshit!"

A strange and maniacal laugh seemed came from the corner of the gym, sending a chill up my spine.

"What on Earth is that?" Zach wondered aloud.

"I think it's coming from the back of the gym," Bryce said.

"Samson, check who that is," Zach instructed.

"Why me?"

"Why not you, tough guy?"

"Fine!"

Samson ran to the source of the laughter, yelling threats and obscenities to whoever was laughing. The laughter stopped. The gym was quiet.

"Samson," Zach yelled.

Out from the darkness of the hallway that led to the gym came Samson, pulling Miguel out by the arm. Miguel was unshaven and disheveled. His clothes were wrinkled. His eyes bloodshot.

"Where— I mean, what happened to you?" Zach asked.

"Not happy to see me?" Miguel said.

Like the others, Zach was dumbfounded. I stood alone among my comrades, who watched Miguel's madness on full display. I'm sure it was heartbreaking for them. I inhaled the dense air. The air conditioner shut off after midnight, and I was hot, feeling the sweat drip off my brow. Not just from the heat, but at the volatility of Miguel, who was capable of doing anything that might compromise me. "Savage," Miguel spat at me.

"Savage?" Zach asked. "Who's a savage?"

"Coop," he said.

"Why is he a savage?" Zach asked.

"Can't you see he's crazy?" I said, wiping sweat from my face.

Miguel tossed an empty chair across the gym floor. It slid and crashed against the bleachers.

Miguel's face turning red. "I am not crazy."

"Coop's just worried about you. We all are," Zach said.

Miguel sprinted to the front of the gym, then to Bryce, pulling his hair and pounding his chest with a closed fist.

"He's a savage!"

Bryce stepped back and quickly left the gym. The door slammed behind him.

"Get him out of here," I told Zach. I left before the rest of the team adjourned. Kayla followed me outside.

"Coop, did you really hit him?" she asked, looking at the pavement. "I'm sorry. Stupid question."

Kayla began walking away before she stopped and faced me. "Will I see you again?" she asked.

The wind blew steadily as another rain band approached from the Gulf. Kayla's long bangs fluttered in the breeze while she squeezed my hand.

"No," I said. I left her in the rain.

# Chapter 19

A few days after the meeting we had a two-game home series against FIU. I hadn't heard from Alison in days. I tried calling her before the first game but she didn't answer. I wished I was starting. I hated sitting in the bullpen waiting for my next start. After game two I tried to call her again. No answer. I went over to her dorm. I knocked on her door. After several attempts, Joanna answered. She had her hands on her sides, her right hip extended outward, her bottom lip tucked underneath the top.

"What do you want?" she asked.

"Where's Alison?" I asked.

"She's not here."

"Where is she? I tried calling but she hasn't answered."

"She doesn't want to see you," Joanna said.

"What? Why?"

"I think you know."

"No, I don't actually."

"Why don't you figure it out, asshole?" she said, slamming the door in my face. I went to leave and nearly tripped over something beside the door. A pair of pink rain boots.

I spent the entire day searching all around campus for her. The Grind, the library, the bookstore. I went back to her dorm and waited outside until nightfall, sitting on a bench, watching students come and go. Suddenly, Alison emerged at the edge of my vision.

"Alison!" I said, running to her. She kept walking as if I wasn't even there. "Hey, would you stop?"

Alison continued on until I stood in front of her, blocking her until she realized I wasn't moving. She rolled her eyes as she clutched her textbooks in her arms.

"What's going on with you?" I said.

"I don't want to talk to you right now."

"Why? Tell me."

"I can't do this."

I took her by the hand and lead her to the open patch of grass and trees that lay in front of her dorm.

" I want to know what's going on. And I want to know right now," I said.

Alison plopped her textbooks on the floor and shoved her finger in my chest. "Joanna saw you two nights ago with Kayla."

I rubbed my forehead in frustration as Alison went on berating me. "It's not what you think, Alison," I said.

"Oh really? She saw you arm-in-arm with that whore."

"Alison. We were looking for Bryce. She just offered to come along."

"Am I that stupid, Coop?"

I was ready to spit her secret in her face. I clenched my fist as I felt it tremble. I stammered as I gave her a cold look.

"Where have you been all day?" I asked. "I looked for you all afternoon."

She shook her head, fighting back her emotions by biting her lip, which quivered before she spoke. "I don't think that's any of your concern, but if you must know, I was with Patrick."

"Buckhorn? Why?" I asked with a scowl.

"What do you care?"

I grabbed her arm. My nails dug into her skin. "Why were you with Buckhorn?"

Alison struggled to free herself from my grip. "Let go of me, Cooper."

"I asked you what you were doing with Buckhorn!"

Alison kept throwing her right arm to break my hold of her. "Cooper, you're hurting me. Let me go." My nails dug in deeper. I didn't see it coming. Her left hand came from nowhere, slapping my face hard with an open palm, getting the attention of a few students who walked by. Alison ran back to her dorm.

"Alison!" I yelled as she left me in the open field.

The fourth floor of our dorm was quiet. Our door was open. I found Bryce sitting on the edge of his bed with his head down and the palm of his hand pressed against his face. He sat out the series against FIU because of a sore shoulder. If he wasn't in his dorm, he would walk around campus by himself. He didn't hear me come in. I closed the door. He looked at me with red, swollen eyes. I pretended not to notice.

I took off my windbreaker and tossed it on the bed. I sat across from him and didn't say a word. He couldn't bear to look at me. For the first time, Bryce found himself alone. In his thoughts, in his mind that was betraying him. I understood how that felt. I pitied him, in a way.

"What's wrong?" I asked standing over him.

He said nothing for a moment, just looking down at the white carpet stained from years of neglect. Bryce's almond shaped eyes were bloodshot, from crying, lack of sleep, or both. "I saw them," Bryce said.

"Who?" I asked.

"I can't believe it … I…."

"Who did you see? Tell me."

"I followed Dawn after the banquet. She walked alone. I followed her to the athletic building. I went inside. He was there. They."

Bryce had difficulty stringing sentences together.

"I saw them together. Dawn and Buckhorn at his office."

"Did they see you?"

"No. The door was closed. But I heard them. I know her moan."

I stood from the bed, a position that made me feel I was towering over Bryce in his moment of vulnerability.

"I knew," I said. "About Dawn and Buckhorn."

Sheer disbelief consumed Bryce as he lifted himself from the bed, grimacing.

"What?"

"I saw them together at her dorm that night I was supposed to talk to her."

He rushed at me and slammed me against the closet. I was no match for him. I just took it as if I was a bystander while he thrust all his weight against me.

"Why didn't you say anything?" Bryce said clenching his teeth.

"It wouldn't have mattered."

He slammed me against the closet again. His right elbow leaving a fist-sized hole in it. He pushed me away and stood by himself in the corner of the room.

"What am I going to do, Coop?," he whispered.

The moment of truth arrived. It swept over me like a cold, delicious wind. All the events leading up to our current circumstance lead to only one conclusion, made deliciously simple.

"What if there was a way we could get rid of Buckhorn?" I said.

Bryce faced me with widened eyes. "Get rid of Buckhorn?"

"Yes."

"How? He's the Athletic Director."

I shrugged. "So?"

"I'll go to Coach about this."

I sat beside him on the bed with my hands folded, watching the nervous energy radiate from his body. I fed off of it like you wouldn't believe. The hairs on the back of my neck stood. It was delightful. "Why? You think it will make a difference?"

"I have to go to somebody about this."

"It won't matter who you go to. Dawn's not going to admit to anything and Buckhorn will deny everything. You'll be risking your reputation all for a lie."

"But it isn't a lie."

"To you, yes, but others won't see it that way. You're taking prescription meds, aren't you?"

Bryce cocked his head. "So?"

"Isn't one of side of effects of Vicodin mental distress? You won't have much of a case."

Bryce stammered and shook his head. "What is all this?" Bryce said.

"What I'm talking about is a way to remove Buckhorn from the picture so that he'll never bother us again. For things to be as they were."

"And how do you propose to do that?"

I grinned and put my hand on his knee. "The same way I took you out of commission last season."

"What?" Bryce jumped.

"You heard me. We have an inter-squad game next week. That will be our chance."

Bryce began biting his thumbnail. His eyes twitched around the room, his brain was a flurry of activity.

"I can't, I mean, I just…."

"What's the alternative? Have Buckhorn running our lives? Taking advantage of people we care about? Is that what you want?"

"There has to be another way."

"There isn't, Bryce," I said, shaking my head.

"How?"

"Buckhorn is too proud. Taunt him during practice when I'm pitching. Tell him he couldn't hit my fastball or some shit like that. Talk smack. He won't be able to resist taking a crack at me."

"And then?"

"I'll take care of the rest. You just need to pretend that nothing happened. Keep it business as usual," I said.

Bryce's head sunk as he shook his head, trying to make sense of it all.

"I don't know if I can."

"Can what?"

"This is too much. I mean. This isn't right."

"The line between right and wrong is pretty vague, Bryce. I wish the world was as black and white as you think it is. But it isn't. Things are never what they seem to be. You'll find that most people end up disappointing you when it's all said and done. I wish it weren't that way. But maybe now we have a chance to change things. To break the rules we didn't have a say in making."

Bryce nodded with a determined glare. "OK."

I suggested he get some sleep. He didn't bother to change, just hid underneath his bed sheets. Bryce fell to sleep instantly.

I turned off the light. He didn't notice me staring at him in the dark, just a silhouette of myself standing over his bed like a specter in the night.

# Chapter 20

It felt like a fall morning, dark and cold, with gusts of wet wind coming in. Zach raked the infield, shuffling the dirt until it was dry enough to use. The outfield was wet with puddles of water along the right field line. It was a miserable day, but Dawson wanted us to get some work in.

We were tied with Georgia for first. The NCAA Division II playoffs were approaching. Bryce and I didn't speak to each other throughout most of practice, just subtle nods of the head and glances that spoke a thousand words.

That morning we did calisthenics. We weren't the most talented team, but we're going to be the most fit team in the league if Dawson had anything to say about it. After doing sprints, push-ups, and a one-mile jog, we began situations.

I didn't pitch first. I warmed up in the bullpen. My arm felt loose, though it was hard to get a grip on the ball in the light drizzle that remained. Buckhorn acted as third base coach. I watched him as I finished my warm-up. I was due to pitch next. I wiped my hand on my pants before I jogged over to the mound. Coach put a runner on first and third with two outs. I threw three straight balls before

Bryce called time and jogged over to the mound. We both covered our mouths with our mitts.

"I don't know about this, Coop," Bryce muffled through his mitt.

"Just remember what we talked about."

"When?"

"There are two outs. I'll get the strikeout and the inning will be over. That's when you'll do it. You're not really getting second thoughts, are you?"

"Maybe we're in over our heads."

"Don't you trust me?"

Coach yelled for us to get a move on. Bryce jogged back to home plate. I threw a fastball right up the middle. Strike one. One on the inside, strike two. He called a change-up. "Strike three!" The umpire, the fielders jogging back to the away dugout.

"Got to work on that control, Coop. You were lucky. Three straight balls," Buckhorn said.

"And three straight strikes."

"True, but we can do better."

"Say, I got an idea, why don't you take a crack at Coop?" Bryce said to Buckhorn.

"You serious?" Buckhorn replied.

"Why not?"

"Wouldn't want to hold up practice."

"Nah. Three pitches."

"What are the stakes?" Buckhorn said.

"Coop strikes you out, you take the entire team out to dinner."

"And If I get a hit?"

"You get a date with Dawn," Bryce joked.

Buckhorn squinted, looking over to Coach Dawson, who tapped his watch to hurry it up.

"If you hit Coop here, we'll give you a Championship dinner at a place of your choice."

Buckhorn looked down and dug his foot in the moist dirt beneath him. "Give me a bat," Buckhorn said.

Bryce picked up a bat off the ground and handed it to him.

Coach, unamused, wanted to know what the hell we were doing.

"Just a friendly wager, Coach," Buckhorn said.

"Wager?"

"Just teaching Coop a thing or two."

"Coop, don't you pitch to him!" Coach yelled.

"Relax, this won't take long," I said waving my glove at coach.

Coach threw his hat against the wall of the dugout.

Buckhorn picked up a helmet from the dugout, put it on, and stepped into the right side of the plate with a slight open stance.

"Give me what you got, Coop," Buckhorn said.

Now it was him and me. We were one in the same. Two competitors trying to show each other up. Adrenaline raced through my veins like I was racehorse ready to jump out of the gate. I could hear my heartbeat thundering in my ears.

I dug my nails deep in the stitching of the ball, just like I'd dug into Alison's skin. I stared at Buckhorn beneath the brim of my hat.

It all happened so fast, faster than when I hit Bryce. It took my breath away, how easy it was. I remember Bryce taking off his catcher's mask and standing over Buckhorn as he lay on the ground, motionless. The ball rolled to the edge of the backstop, a smudge of blood mixed with the red stitching of the ball.

I waited in Coach Dawson's office, away from the madness that consumed the field after I hit Buckhorn in the skull. There was no word of his condition, only that he was unconscious. I was still in uniform. I was unsure of where Bryce was, as I'd been told to report to Coach Dawson's office immediately.

I waited there alone for several hours. My mind was a blank, just a cover of blackness engulfing my mind. Not even a sliver of remorse or guilt. I lay down on Dawson's couch. Again, nothing but an empty void when I closed my eyes. I was startled when the door suddenly swung open.

Dawson sat down in his chair and rubbed his forehead. He kept tapping his finger on his desk.

I sat on the couch, dazed, an outside observer, as though I wasn't even myself anymore.

"Do you have anything to say?"

I shrugged looking down at my hands as I cracked my knuckles. Dawson shook his head and interlaced his fingers.

"He's still unconscious and in critical condition. Doctors don't know for how long." Dawson lifted himself off his desk and leaned over me, his face inches from mine. "Do you understand what I am telling you?" he asked, veins popping out from his forehead.

I nodded yes, remaining mute.

"Do you have anything to say, Coop?"

"I don't think there's anything else to say, Coach."

He sat next to me. His hands gripped his knees, joining the momentary silence. "I know that neither of us liked Buckhorn. But what happened out there today … I don't want to think about the hows and the whys of what occurred out on that field. I just can't explain it. And to be honest, I'm not sure if I want to." He inhaled a deep breath and put his hand on my knee. "I'm suspending you as of today."

I gently bobbed my head against the wall, the beat thudding through the silence in the room.

"Is it your call?"

"The pressure's coming from up top. I had to do it."

"What about the playoffs? The championship?"

"I can't have another disaster like what happened out there today and last year. I have no choice in the matter. This a huge shit storm, Coop. I tried to convince Janet otherwise. But she's in damage control mode. This is much bigger than just baseball. We're talking about the future of the school here, and they're not going to put the school's future in jeopardy over accidents like this."

Dawson sat in his chair and turned on the desk fan. The drone from the fan hummed as cool air blew in his face.

"I'll keep you informed of Buckhorn's condition," he said.

The rain subsided. The afternoon was hot and humid as the storm moved further east, though there were still gusts of wind that blustered through the confines of the campus grounds.

# Chapter 21

Dawson suggested not to visit Buckhorn in the hospital, but I wasn't really interested in going back anyways. Several times was enough in Bryce's case.

I hadn't seen Bryce in a few days. He left with the team for a three-game series. I spent most of my time wandering around campus for hours, skipping class, hoping no one would notice me. I visited Brass field. The gate to the stadium was open. I stood by the dugout and stared at the mound. I knew from that point on my baseball career was over. The little sliver of hope that pushed me these past four years vanished out of thin air. Now I was a nobody. A has-been, or better yet, a never was. I never lived up to my potential. Instead I was living under a shadow that now swallowed me whole. I walked to the mound, my throwing hand trembled with every step I took.

I stopped mid-way, looking at the sky before I fell on my knees. My chest tightened. I thought I couldn't breath. I wrapped my arms around myself, rocking back and forth hoping the pain would go away. After a few minutes I picked myself back up, swearing I would never return to Brass Field and enter the real world and face the unknown. I came to the conclusion that school was just a big joke, and Tampa State was getting the last laugh.

I called Alison dozens of times only to get her voicemail. I was too afraid to show up at her dorm. I imagined Alison opening her dorm room door with that smile of hers, embracing me, kissing me, telling me everything would be OK. Finally she answered my phone call. My skin crawled when she answered as if she didn't know me. I asked her if we could meet. The silence felt louder than a blow horn before she agreed to meet me in front of The Grind.

It was filled with students in desperate need of caffeine to fuel their all-nighters. She was beautiful even with bags under her eyes, her face without any make-up. I blushed when I saw her. If only I could figure out a way to make her smile again.

I offered her a cup of coffee but she declined. We sat outside. Her hair waved in the breeze. Looking at her, it made me sick. I offered to buy her coffee and pastries again. She shook her head, not even taking a glance at me. I began with small talk. I asked her about her day and how finals were going, but she ignored every question. Nothing I said brought back the Alison I knew. I was beginning to lose her right in front of my eyes.

"I don't think we should see each other anymore," she said avoiding eye contact.

I took a deep breath. "I wasn't myself. I've been under a lot of stress."

Alison shook her head. Her eyes were watery. "Is that all you have to say … stress?"

I played with the lid of my coffee cup. "Apologizing won't make much of a difference. I know that."

She wiped her eyes with her hands. "Did you mean to hit him?"

Spit seemed to get lodged in my throat. For a moment I thought I couldn't swallow, that I was going to suffocate from my own saliva.

"I thought you should know he came on to me," Alison said, as if I didn't already know.

My chest constricted, tightening with every minute she stayed near me.

"Don't you want to know what I did?" she asked.

My chin quivered, my body paralyzed, unable to say a coherent word or phrase.

"Do you even care?" she added. "I told him I had a boyfriend and I threatened to inform the school authorities. Nothing happened. He just played dumb and changed the conversation to what I was doing over the summer. He acted like a little kid who got in trouble by his parents. Then I left"

I stared directly into her eyes. "I saw you at the frat party Alison. I saw you up go those stairs with him that night."

Alison rubbed her eyes and shook her head. "I don't think I have anything more to say to you."

She picked up her purse from the chair. "Goodbye, Cooper." She pressed her lips to my cheek. I didn't even watch her leave, just listening to the fading of her footsteps as she left.

# Chapter 22

When I got back to the dorm, Bryce was there, sitting on his bed with a face of stone.

"Hey, Bryce," I said. I could tell he was shivering. "You alright?"

He sat there without muttering a word.

"Say, why don't we get a bite to eat? My treat?" I said.

Bryce paced around the room, running his hands through his hair.

"Not hungry?" I said.

"No," Bryce said grabbing his catcher's mitt from his nightstand, sliding it in his left hand and breaking it in with his right fist, punching the palm of the glove tell his knuckles were red.

"I'm not on the team anymore."

Bryce nodded and continued pounding his mitt with his fist, looking at me with swollen eyes, like he's been crying for hours.

"Is it Dawn?"

*Pop.Pop.Pop.* His fist hit the glove, each punch harder than the last. He slid his mitt off and dropped on the floor and sat on the corner of the bed. A silence ensued. I leaned against the wall, hitting the back of my head against it.

"He's dead," Bryce spat.

My throat felt clogged again. "What?"

Bryce turned his head, surprised of my ignorance. "You didn't hear?"

"No. When?"

"This morning. School's being all hush-hush about it." Bryce looked up at me. "What did we do, Coop? We killed him."

I rushed to Bryce and pointed my finger at him. "We didn't do a damn thing."

"But ... the plan?"

"What plan? I don't recall there being a plan," I said, standing over him. "It was an accident. That's all."

"Liar!" He threw his mitt across the room. "That's not what happened. It wasn't supposed to happen like this. You were just supposed to just hurt him."

Tears dripped down his face. Every tear enraged me further. He acted like a victim, pretending he had nothing to do with it, trying to be the "better man." My hand trembled, but I didn't bother fighting it anymore. I stretched my arm back and hit him repeatedly with my open hand, his cheek turning red. He just sat there and did nothing. One slap after the other, like his fist smacking the palm of his glove. I felt Bryce's tears rinse through the palm of my hand

"You moron," I said, smacking him one last time. "You're not innocent in all of this. You knew what was going to happen. Didn't you see it?"

"How could I?"

"Don't you even remember what happened last year?"

Bryce tried to say something but he mumbled his words in a incoherent dribble, enraging me further.

I paced around the room with my heart ready to jump out of my chest. "What happened last year wasn't an accident."

Bryce cocked his head back in confusion before he let out a weak laugh. "Seriously, Coop, you're losing it."

"I'm serious," I said.

His grin disappeared. I thought he was going to cry again. I could see his eyes swell up.

"Look, it was an accident. Everybody knows that. Coach—"

"Shut up! Listen to me. What happened last year wasn't an accident. You know why? Because I meant to hit you, Bryce. I threw that ball right at your fucking head. And you wanna know something else? I didn't think twice about it. I liked it."

"Stop it," Bryce said.

"It wasn't an accident," I said.

"I said stop."

I clenched my fists. "I meant to hit you. Do you understand what I'm telling you?"

"Stop!"

He trembled uncontrollably while I stood over him like a dark shadow.

"I thought we were friends," he said with a cracked voice.

I scoffed. "You're so naive."

"Weren't we? I just want to know. Please?"

I shrugged. Zach stormed into the room with that damn robe of his. "What's happening here? I heard yelling."

Zach took a quick look at Bryce and turned his attention to me. "What did you do?"

I simply grinned and left the dorm room.

I walked down the hall and heard a scuffle in the room between Zach and Bryce. "Calm down." I glanced back down the hall to find Bryce standing there in the middle of the hallway.

"Coop, please! Weren't we? Don't do this to me!"

Zach had to hold him back from chasing me. I left Orsini Hall and never looked back.

# Epilogue

I felt my knees ache and shoulder twinge as I walked back onto James Brass Field, all those years after I graduated. I didn't bother going to the ceremony. I left the diploma in the closet of my old bedroom where it still sits to this day, almost forgotten. Now, fifteen years later, I remember the carnage I inflicted on so many people. I lost friendship, I lost love, I lost the innocence that comes with youth.

That monster still hides in the shadow of my soul, from time to time resurfacing to show its ugly head. Sometimes I would dream about Alison and think I'm back in her dorm, lying next to her, like time doesn't matter.

There are worse dreams. One where I see Buckhorn's bloody face lying on the ground, black swollen eyes staring back at me. His face haunts me like the memories that linger on, even as I get older and slip into mediocrity. I wonder what life could've been. If I'd never succumbed to my demons. If I'd just acted like everyone else. But I am a member of the dead, walking among the living, wandering and imagining what could have been.

Strolling around the third base line, I noticed a baseball near the dugout. Its' leather was scuffed and covered with dirt. I picked it up and tossed it in the air, my fingers gripping the red leather stitching.

Frank Nunez

It felt good to pick up a baseball again, whiffing the smell of dirt and grass off the ball brought me back to when I actually mattered.

    I walked to the mound and pressed my back foot against the rubber. I leaned forward, ready to get in my deliver. My nails dug into the leather, causing my skin to tingle from the adrenaline and euphoria that rushed through me. For a moment I saw Bryce poised in the batter's box, his naiveté and ignorance oozing through him, like the dark red blood from his eyes. I knew the pitch I wanted to throw. My hand began to shake as my nails dug deeper. I got in the stretch, my front foot lifted off the ground, my windup fluid with my arm whipping towards home plate. I saw Bryce's face as I released the ball, and all I could do was smile.

The End